THE WEAPONS OF OUR WARFARE

The Weapons of our Warfare

'Blessed be the LORD my strength, which teacheth my hands to war, and my fingers to fight'
Psalm 144:1

Francis Wale Oke

Highland
Guildford, Surrey

Copyright © 1994 Francis Wale Oke

British Library Cataloguing-in-Publication Data. A catalogue
record for this book is available from the British Library

Published by Highland, an imprint of Inter Publishing Service
(IPS) Ltd, 59 Woodbridge Road, Guildford, Surrey GU1 4RF.

Also published in Nigeria by:
Victory Literature Crusade
Akunleyan Estate
Opposite Green Spring Hotel
Old Ife Road
PO Box 6308
Agodi PO
IBADAN

Victory Literature Crusade
25 Belmont Avenue
Tottenham
London N17 6AX

Typeset by The Electronic Book Factory Ltd, Fife
Printed in the UK by HarperCollins Manufacturing, Glasgow.

ISBN 1 897913 15 X

This book is prayerfully dedicated
to Isaac, my son, trusting the Lord
to fulfil what He spoke about you
before you were born.

The Weapons

'It is true that I am an ordinary weak human being, but I don't use human plans and methods to win my battles. I use God's mighty weapons, not those made by men, to knock down the devil's strongholds. These weapons can break down every proud argument against God and every wall that can be built to keep men from finding him. With these weapons I can capture rebels and bring them back to God, and change them into men whose hearts' desire is obedience to Christ. I will use these weapons against every rebel who remains after I have first used them on you yourselves, and you surrender to Christ.'

2 Corinthians 10:3–6 (LB)

'For though we walk in the flesh, we do not war after the flesh: (for the weapons of our warfare are not carnal, but mighty through God to the pulling down of strong holds;) casting down imaginations, and every high thing that exalteth itself against the knowledge of God, and bringing into captivity every thought to the obedience of Christ; and having in a readiness to revenge all disobedience, when your obedience is fulfilled.'

2 Corinthians 10:3–6 (KJV)

Contents

Foreword

Several books have been written on spiritual warfare. Many of them are straightforward expositions of scriptures, such as Ephesians 6:10–18. These are helpful and beneficial to the believer. This book comes from the pen of a Bible expositor and a 'practitioner'. Here is a man who writes with a pen in one hand and a sword in the other. He puts the principles he writes about into practice each day as he faces the ferocity of satanic opposition in his evangelistic crusades in Nigeria. Here, on a daily basis, he encounters the works of darkness and overcomes them.

Francis Wale Oke is a young Nigerian evangelist who draws multi-thousands of non-Christians to his successful evangelistic crusades. He is in great demand also as a conference speaker, and hundreds of ministers from all denominations are greatly helped by his biblical and practical expositions. I have been with him in some of his crusades in Africa and I am left in no doubt that God has raised him to play a crucial role in gathering the end-time harvest on that great continent. I remember in particular a pastors conference he called in 1990 where I was a guest speaker. It blessed me to see church leaders from all the states of Nigeria and a few other African nations come together to be taught and challenged to take the continent for Jesus through

in-depth evangelism. I am happy he has put into writing some of the principles the Lord has taught him. I
believe these materials will be a blessing to you.

                          Wynne Lewis
                          General Superintendent,
                          Elim Pentecostal Missions.

Introduction

The Christian is continuously engaged in spiritual warfare. This battle goes on every day, mostly in the unseen realm. Though very often we have it manifested in the physical, in the real sense it is a spiritual warfare.

You are involved in a spiritual warfare. You have to know the weapons God has provided for you to fight and start to apply them diligently. Then and only then will you be able to overcome the devil and all his hosts, and realise God's purpose for your life.

Billy Graham once said 'God is not calling us to a playground or a sports arena. He is calling us to a battle-ground. This struggle is worldwide and unavoidable.'

As you brace yourself with the fact of spiritual battle and you start to 'fight the good fight of faith', you are no longer a victim but a victor. You start living in high victory and all fears give way in your life. You start becoming a blessing to others. Then God will be glorified and the enemy totally defeated in your life.

David, the great warrior and prophetic king of Israel said: *'Blessed be the LORD my strength, which teacheth my hands to war, and my fingers to fight'* (Psalm 144:1).

That is exactly what God wants to do with you, using

this book. He wants to teach your hands to war and fingers to fight.

I am very sure that by knowing and applying the spiritual principles set out in this book you will be able to assert your authority over the hosts of hell and be able to say boldly that you are more than a conqueror.

May the blessings of the Lord rest upon this book wherever it goes ... in the name of Jesus Christ our Lord. Amen.

Francis Wale Oke
Ibadan 1994

Chapter One
Spiritual Warfare

The Bible does not keep us in the dark at all concerning spiritual warfare. God makes it abundantly clear that we are at war and shows us the way to overcome and be *'more than conquerors'* (Romans 8:37). From Genesis to Revelation we are made to know that spiritual warfare is a daily and continuous reality. *'For we wrestle . . .'* (Ephesians 6:12).

Wrestling! That is what we do continuously. Not playing but fighting. Not resting but wrestling.

Fight the good fight of faith, lay hold on eternal life, whereunto thou art also called, and hast professed a good profession before many witnesses.

(I Timothy 6:12)

We are told here again to fight the good fight of faith. Eternal life is at stake; lay hold of it as a present possession.

God is real. The devil is real. The struggle between evil and good is real also. You need to realise this and have a right attitude to spiritual warfare so you can be a winner now and in the end.

The enemies we are fighting against are not human beings. The Bible says *'For though we walk in the*

flesh, we do not war after the flesh' (II Corinthians
10:3). Our enemies are spiritual beings. Many people
think they are to use their spiritual weapons against
human beings. But what does Scripture say?

> *For we wrestle not against flesh and blood, but*
> *against principalities, against powers, against the*
> *rulers of the darkness of this world, against spir-*
> *itual wickedness in high places.*
>
> (Ephesians 6:12)

Here, our enemies are clearly identified and put into
four categories. Principalities, powers, rulers of the
darkness of this world, spiritual wickedness in high
places.

These are malevolent spirits who direct their dia-
bolical activities against us. They put obstacles in the
way of our spiritual progress. They are responsible for
spiritual blindness, ignorance and unbelief. They seek
to hinder us from being prosperous and fruitful. They
try to weaken our hands and render us ineffective in the
service of God's Kingdom. They bring discouragement,
sin, fear and doubts if we allow them to.

They want to keep a child of God in bondage in
spite of the unlimited spiritual authority each child
has over them through the name of Jesus. Given the
opportunity, they would draw back a Christian from
following the Lord.

Physical sicknesses, diseases and oppressions have
their origin in Satan. Moral defilements, wrong doctrines, mental sicknesses and emotional afflictions,
ultimately come from him also. Infidelity and unfaith-
fulness in marriage, marital problems and crises, as
well as divorce, are traceable to demonic interference
in the life of man.

These demonic forces, by influencing men, are responsible for all the calamities in the world today.

When man was made by God in the beginning, he had no problem whatsoever. Man was made in the image of God, blessed and endowed with authority and dominion over all living things as well as the whole creation. He was *very good* (Genesis 1:31). But the very day man first committed sin, the devil came in with his host of demons. Since then, problems and calamities have become a part of the human race. Satan and his demons are behind them all.

Ignorance Is Deadly

These powers of darkness always capitalise on ignorance as they work in the lives of people. That is why ignorance is a very perilous thing for a child of God. *My people are destroyed for lack of knowledge* (Hosea 4:6).

To be ignorant of the fact that we are fighting a spiritual war daily is to be a victim of the devil. To be ignorant of the devices of the enemy is to be easily susceptible to defeat.

To be ignorant of the weapons that the Lord has provided for His people, and not to make effective use of them is to go about in fear, unable to fight an effective battle. We must realise we are at war. We must know our enemies – their strength and limitations, their weaknesses and how to overcome them. We must know the weapons of war that we have and how to skilfully use them.

Many people think life is a game of chances, of trial and error. They suppose that whatever happens is

purely accidental. This is not so. There is a cause and
an effect to everything that happens in life. Negative
things do not just happen by chance. They have a
spiritual cause. That is why we must be on the winning
side if we will win in life. To be on the side of Jesus
Christ of Nazareth is to be on the winning side.

Many others think that life is a matter of destiny.
'Whatever will be will be, no matter what you do,'
they say. There is no bigger lie the devil has devised
to keep men out of the best in life. The whole universe
is governed by definite divine laws. There are physical
laws and there are spiritual laws. If you discover the
prevailing law and operate according to it, you win. It is
in the Bible that spiritual laws that govern the universe
are explained. God governs the whole universe by His
Word. The Bible says that Jesus Christ upholds all
things by the Word of His power (Hebrews 1:3). When
you know the truth of the Word of God, you discover the
laws that govern the whole universe. And Jesus Christ
has said that the truth that you know will make you
free (John 8:36).

The law of the LORD is perfect, converting the
*   soul:*
The testimony of the LORD is sure, making wise
*   the simple.*
The statutes of the LORD are right, rejoicing the
*   heart:*
The commandment of the LORD is pure,
*   enlightening the eyes.*
The fear of the LORD is clean, enduring for
*   ever:*
The judgments of the LORD are true and righteous
*   altogether.*

*   (Psalm 19:7–9.)*

Other people think a man must always struggle and
live by the product of his struggles. This is only partially
true. We need to do more than struggle to be victorious
in life. We need Jesus. We need to rely on Him and trust
Him completely. When we do that our struggles cease
and our victory begins. The Lord then begins to direct
our paths and every step we take.

Trust in the LORD with all thine heart;
and lean not unto thine own understanding.
In all thy ways acknowledge him,
and he shall direct thy paths.

(Proverbs 3:5–6)

Commit thy works unto the Lord,
and thy thoughts shall be established.

(Proverbs 16:3)

Absolute reliance on God is the pathway to breakthrough and accomplishment. As we rely on Him, He
begins to direct our paths and every step we take. He
begins to give us victories and blessings that are clearly
beyond human struggles and sweats.

The blessing of the LORD, it maketh rich,
And he addeth no sorrow with it.

(Proverbs 10:22)

So then it is not of him that willeth, nor of him
that runneth, but of God that sheweth mercy.

(Romans 9:16)

The following words by E. W. Kenyon are both true and
appropriate:

I cannot conceive how successful work can be
done today, or how believers can be in place

of continual victory, unless they know that the
source of their danger lies in demonical power,
and that the power to conquer it is in the Name
of Jesus of Nazareth, the Son of God. The more
quickly we recognise that the very air about is
filled with hostile forces, who are attempting to
destroy our fellowship with the Father, and to
deprive us of our usefulness in the service of our
Master, the better it will be for us.[1]

Stand Up And Be Counted

Many Christians do not want to fight any battle. They
are neither willing to face challenges nor ready to
deal with the problems that come their way. Many
are always looking for the path of least resistance,
running away from whatever poses a problem. They
compromise and fret; they are ever anxious, ever fearful, ever worried, ever complaining. This was the case
with the Israelites in the wilderness. Their story is told
in Numbers 13 and 14. They saw the giants in the land
the Lord had promised to deliver into their hands, but
instead of trusting the Lord and fighting the battle,
they ran away, complaining and grumbling that they
could not possess the land. Only Joshua and Caleb had
the courage and boldness to fight the battle, and they
inherited the promise. The others refused to fight; they
perished and did not obtain the promise. Their fears
and doubts ensnared them.

We are warned not to follow their example of unbelief. We are, rather, to follow those who fought the
good fight of faith and who through faith and patience
inherited the blessings of God.

*That ye be not slothful, but followers of them who
through faith and patience inherit the promises.*

(Hebrews 6:12)

Stand up today and be counted in God's end-time army.
Prepare for war. Be set for victory. There is a definite
inheritance God has prepared for you these end-times.
You should be ready to possess your inheritance by
getting involved in spiritual warfare.

Satan Defeated

One very important point we must not be ignorant of,
which we must have always on our mind is this: the devil
and all his hosts are a bunch of defeated foes, totally and
completely defeated by the Lord Jesus Christ. The Bible
says they are already spoilt (paralysed) by Jesus.

*And having spoiled principalities and powers, he
made a shew of them openly, triumphing over
them in it.*

(Colossians 2:15)

He paralysed them completely and triumphed openly
over them. Our clear understanding of this fact is a
vital key to our victory. Never should you be afraid of
the devil; he is a defeated foe. However, we are not to
take him for granted. That is the purpose of this book.
Let us examine some more scriptures on this.

*Forasmuch then as the children are partakers of
flesh and blood, he also himself likewise took part
of the same; that through death he might destroy
him that had the power of death, that is, the devil;*

and deliver them who through fear of death were
all their lifetime subject to bondage.

(Hebrews 2:14–15)

Jesus Christ became flesh for one purpose – that He
might destroy the devil who had the power of death,
and liberate us completely from all that Satan uses to
keep us bound. This He did by His death on the cross
of Calvary and His glorious resurrection on the third
day. No wonder He said on the cross *'It is finished'*
(John 19:30). Redemption work is finished. The defeat
of Satan is accomplished. Total deliverance now is
available to all who believe.

Howbeit we speak wisdom among them that are
perfect: yet not the wisdom of this world, nor of
the princes of this world, that come to nought ...
Which none of the princes of this world knew: for
had they known it, they would not have crucified
the Lord of glory.

(I Corinthians 2:6–8)

Here the Bible refers to the *'princes of this world'* and
that they have *'come to nought'*. Our Lord Jesus Christ
made it clear that the devil is the *'prince of this world'*
(John 14:30). It is the devil and his hosts that constitute
'the princes of this world' that *'have come to nought'*.
They did not know that in the wisdom of God, Jesus
was to defeat and vanquish them all through His death
and resurrection. Had they known, they would not have
incited the people to crucify Him. But Jesus has died
and has risen. He has defeated the devil and his hosts
forever. Satan is a defeated foe.

The devil is defeated. His defeat is so total, he can
do nothing about it. The victory of Jesus over him was

complete and everlasting. Nothing can be taken from it and nothing can be added to it. The devil has no longer either power or authority over any child of God. He only has 'wiles', 'devices' and cunning craftiness. We are to be aware of all his wiles and devices, and overcome them all using the weapons of our warfare. Be strong therefore, and be bold. Be strong in the Lord and prepare for battle. That is how you obtain your inheritance and possess your possession:

> *Finally, my brethren, be strong in the Lord, and in the power of his might. Put on the whole armour of God, that ye may be able to stand against the wiles of the devil. For we wrestle not against flesh and blood, but against principalities ... against spiritual wickedness in high places. Wherefore take unto you the whole armour of God, that ye may be able to withstand in the evil day, and having done all, to stand.*
>
> (Ephesians 6:10–13)

A Fight Of Faith

This battle is a 'fight of faith'. It is by faith we overcome. *'Fight the good fight of faith'* (I Timothy 6:12).

Faith is the victory that overcomes. The 'giants' on your way may be big and out of proportion. The 'mountain' on your path might have been well-established for years. The 'sycamore tree' in your life may be deeply rooted. Yet, all these shall give way when we fight the good fight of faith. Faith is the victory that overcomes in all situations. You are born to reign. You are born to be more than a conqueror. Have this attitude of faith as you begin to make use of our weapons of war.

For whatsoever is born of God overcometh the world: and this is the victory that overcometh the world, even our faith.

(I John 5:4)

The reason for our victory is that someone has won the victory on our behalf: Jesus Christ the Lord. We are only to exercise our faith to enforce this victory He won at Calvary over our enemies. When we do this intelligently, the enemy must run. That is why winning does not depend on any other thing but in our being strong in the Lord. You are not to be strong in yourself.

You are not to be discouraged by the defeats you have suffered in the past. You are not to consider how small you look, or your seeming weaknesses, like the Israelites did. Look to the Lord, instead. Fear not. Only be strong in His grace. Then, *'Resist the devil and he will flee from you'* (James 4:7).

Thou therefore, my son, be strong in the grace that is in Christ Jesus.

(II Timothy 2:1)

God Is Raising His End-Time Army

We are in the last days. Events around the world clearly indicate that the end is near.

God is raising an end-time army. These are the people He will use to deal with the enemy and to consummate His plan for this age. These are a people truly born again and committed to Jesus Christ as their Lord. A people completely delivered from every

demonic hang up and really filled and energised by the
Holy Spirit. A people ready to lay down their lives and
substances for the expansion of His Kingdom. This is
the company of the overcomers.

These are the people He will equip with special anointing and spiritual abilities to deal with the enemy these
last days. They are to bring the saints to maturity and
the Church to perfection. They will be used to deliver
men and women from the shackles of Satan in any form,
bringing them to the saving knowledge of Christ. These
people will learn to use spiritual weapons to deal with
the devil and demonstrate the lordship of Jesus Christ.
They are those who will make the Lord's enemies His
footstool.

> The LORD said unto my Lord, Sit thou at my
>   right hand,
> Until I make thine enemies thy footstool.
> The LORD shall send the rod of thy strength out
>   of Zion:
> Rule thou in the midst of thine enemies.
> Thy people shall be willing in the day of thy
>   power,
> In the beauties of holiness from the womb of the
>   morning:
> Thou hast the dew of thy youth.
>
> (Psalm 110:1–3)

God wants you to be one of these people. All you need
to do is to respond to His call as Isaiah did when he saw
the glory of the Lord and was deeply shaken. He saw
his own unworthiness and filthiness, but deep down
within he was willing to do the will of God. God saw
this and responded to his sincerity. Isaiah was cleansed
and purged of every filth and made worthy of the Lord's

use. Then came the call: *'Whom shall I send, and who will go for us?'* (Isaiah 6:8).

The Lord took a hold of Isaiah, equipped him with divine power and used him beyond description. What a great prophet he became! What a mighty weapon in the hand of the Lord against the kingdom of darkness! All this happened because he made himself available. And that is all you need to do. You do not need to consider yourself, your education, your background or your past. Yield yourself to the Lord completely. Stand up to be counted in the end-time army of God. Then you will see how He will cleanse you, and clothe you with His divine power, and use you greatly for His glory.

For the eyes of the LORD run to and fro throughout the whole earth, to shew himself strong in the behalf of them whose heart is perfect toward him.

(II Chronicles 16:9)

Chapter Two
Adequate Provision

God does not just leave His children to fight the enemy alone. Neither does He ask us to fight in our strength or with carnal weapons. If this were so then there is not a chance in a million that we could win this battle of life. No single human being can overcome the devil in his own strength. But the Lord has made adequate provision. All that we need to succeed in this warfare has been provided. There is no reason why a child of God should be defeated in life. We only need to discover and use effectively what God has provided for us.

There are many people of God today who are being tormented and 'destroyed' by the enemy out of ignorance. Ignorance is deadly. The Bible is very clear on this.

> *Therefore my people are gone into captivity, because they have no knowledge: and their honourable men are famished, and their multitude dried up with thirst.*

(Isaiah 5:13)

This should not be your case at all. Be convinced. God has ordained your victory. You are more than a conqueror in Christ. Step out of ignorance and defeat, into

the glorious liberty of the sons of God. As we examine
God's provision for our victory, let your heart respond
in faith. Begin to possess your possession today.

Jesus Christ has conquered the enemy. He spoilt
principalities and powers and He made an open show
of them. He rose from the dead triumphantly and
ascended into heaven. He is now at the right hand
of the Father interceding for us. With His intercession
we know we are sure to prevail and overcome.

*Wherefore he [Jesus] is able also to save them to
the uttermost that come unto God by him, seeing
he ever liveth to make intercession for them.*
(Hebrews 7:25)

While Jesus was here on earth, He was tempted in all
points just as we are being tempted now, but without
sin. He is conversant and familiar with our problems.
He knows our weaknesses. He feels with us in our
afflictions and trials. And now at the right hand of
the Father, He is our faithful and compassionate High
Priest, who lifts us up when we stumble.

*For in that he himself hath suffered being tempted,
he is able to succour them that are tempted.*
(Hebrews 2:18)

That we have a great High Priest like this is another
marvellous provision of the Father to ensure our ulti-
mate victory in this battle of life.

Protective Covering

Have you seen an army provided with guns, missiles
and diverse offensive weapons but without any protective covering? Infantry men with guns in their hands

but no peculiar dress, no helmet to cover the head, no shoes to protect the feet. Just the weapons. Yet they are going to war. Mark it, these men may succeed in killing some of the enemy but they shall soon be finished, because although they are 'armed to the teeth', they are not protected at all.

Our Father God is wiser than men. He has not only provided us with effective weapons of war but also has for us an impenetrable protective covering – the whole armour of God (Ephesians 6:10–18). This makes us to be well-protected and shielded from the fiery darts of the enemy. We should always put the armour of God on by faith and get ready to fight the enemy. *'Put on the whole armour of God, that ye may be able to stand against the wiles of the devil'* (Ephesians 6:11).

After putting on the whole armour of God and learning how to use our weapons of war, we still need divine strength for accomplishment. It is not by might nor by power that we overcome, but by the Spirit of God. Thanks be to God, the Spirit of Christ is in you, giving you strength and inspiration so you can say: *'I can do all things through Christ which strengtheneth me'* (Philippians 4:13). The Amplified Bible puts it this way:

> *I have strength for all things in Christ who empowers me – I am ready for anything and equal to anything through Him who infuses inner strength into me, (that is, I am self-sufficient in Christ's sufficiency).*
>
> (Philippians 4:13 Amplified Bible)

This is another wonderful provision of our Father. When you make Christ's sufficiency your sufficiency you are harnessing this provision and the result will be that you are being strengthened and empowered to cope with whatever situation you might face in life.

Reigning With Christ As Kings

When Christ rose from the dead, we rose with Him. We ascended with Him to the right hand of the Father. Now we are seated with Him in the heavenly places, where we rule and reign with Christ, exercising spiritual authority over all principalities and powers.

And [God] hath raised us up together, and made us sit together in heavenly places in Christ Jesus: . . .

Far above all principality, and power, and might, and dominion, and every name that is named, not only in this world, but also in that which is to come.
(Ephesians 2:6; 1:21)

From this vantage point, all things are under our feet and we, therefore, can readily enforce the victory of Calvary on the enemy. This is a provision of God.

Having all these provisions, we should lay hold of our weapons of war and fight the good fight of faith. We should not be like the children of Ephraim who turned their back in the day of battle even when they were fully armed. Let us press into our victory. Let us press into our inheritance. Let us awake from our slumber and put on the strength of the Lord.

Awake, awake; put on thy strength, O Zion; put on thy beautiful garments, O Jerusalem, the holy city: for henceforth there shall no more come into thee the uncircumcised and the unclean.
(Isaiah 52:1)

We Are Not Alone

There is another beautiful thing about this spiritual warfare – we are not alone. No matter what the situation or circumstances; no matter how fierce the battle, the Lord of Hosts Himself is with us. He has promised never to leave nor forsake us. When He is in the boat, no storm can turn it over. When He is in the fire, the flame cannot burn even a strand of our hair. Everything is all right when He is there. And He is always there. That is another provision of the Almighty God.

And, lo, I am with you alway, even unto the end of the world. Amen.

(Matthew 28:20b)

Let your conversation be without covetousness; and be content with such things as ye have: for he hath said, I will never leave thee, nor forsake thee. So that we may boldly say,
The Lord is my helper, and I will not fear
What man shall do unto me.

(Hebrews 13:5–6)

Chapter Three

The Weapons Of Our Warfare

God has given us certain weapons to use to overcome the enemy and to raze his kingdom. Let us examine certain things about these weapons.

> *For though we walk in the flesh, we do not war after the flesh: (for the weapons of our warfare are not carnal, but mighty through God to the pulling down of strong holds;) casting down imaginations, and every high thing that exalteth itself against the knowledge of God, and bringing into captivity every thought to the obedience of Christ; and having in a readiness to revenge all disobedience, when your obedience is fulfilled.*
>
> (II Corinthians 10:3–6)

We can see here that these weapons are *'mighty through God'*. One translation says they have *'divine power'*. Because they are of divine origin they must have divine power, hence they are irresistible. Nothing can stand in their way if effectively used. They cast down imaginations, they pull down strongholds, they bring into captivity every thought to the obedience of Christ (note the word 'every'). Nothing Satan can ever devise or imagine can stand against these weapons of war, if correctly applied. This actually lifts us into a realm of abiding victory.

The weapons are very effective. They can deal properly with present problems and revenge all disobedience or rebellion. There is no way the devil can do anything and get away with it.

I remember a brother whose wife had lost an advanced pregnancy and there was such an emotional pressure on the family. While interceding for this family the Spirit of the Lord laid it strongly on my heart that by using our spiritual authority we can force the devil to pay back what he has stolen, a hundredfold. I put pressure on the devil, in the name of the Lord, by the use of our spiritual weapons. And indeed the devil more than paid for what he had done. The Lord used the problem to help the couple understand Him more, and He prepared them to minister more effectively to others who were having similar problems. When our obedience is complete the Lord is ready to take vengeance on our adversaries and give us the victory.

The weapons of our warfare cannot be overcome or rendered useless, and they can never be outdated. They have divine power. This divine power causes them to be ever effective, unconquerable and irresistible.

Many years ago a machine gun was a terribly dreaded weapon. While it is true a machine gun is still very useful, it cannot be compared to a hydrogen bomb. But there is no spiritual weapon that can outclass these that the Almighty God has provided for us.

These weapons are mighty through God. Their effectiveness is not based on man, so that certain Christians can use these weapons while others cannot. Being born again makes you qualified to use the weapons. Faith in God and not in yourself triggers them off. And they work effectually on your behalf.

Ours

These weapons are for us. They are the weapons of *our* warfare. God does not just lock them up somewhere, away from His children. They are available for our use. They are meant for us. As you read this book, you will realise that the weapons are readily available for your use right now.

> *Say not in thine heart, Who shall ascend into heaven? (that is, to bring Christ down from above:) or, Who shall descend into the deep? (that is, to bring up Christ again from the dead.) But what saith it? The word is nigh thee, even in thy mouth, and in thy heart: that is, the word of faith, which we preach.*
>
> (Romans 10:6–8)

No Christian can live victoriously without the effective use of these spiritual weapons. Nobody can overcome the battle of life without using them. We do not need to go about life as one boxing the air. We do not need to be afflicted by the enemy, oppressed and tormented as if God has not made provision for our victory. We should prepare to possess our possession by using the weapons God has provided us with. Prepare to be an overcomer.

Someone might say, 'I have learnt of these things before. I have applied them; but I missed God. I went out of His will and went into sin. And now my chance is gone.' Do not listen to the lies of the devil. You might have missed God. You might have sinned against Him. You might have ignored His will. Yet He still has provision for you. He wants to have you back with Him, to restore you in love. Just confess your sins and allow Him to forgive and cleanse you. Accept His forgiveness and forget the past. Move ahead with faith towards the higher calling He has for you. Do not live in the past. God is the God of the present.

> *If we confess our sins, he is faithful and just to forgive us our sins, and to cleanse us from all unrighteousness.*
>
> (I John 1:9)

Note that God ties His faithfulness and justice to your forgiveness and cleansing. It is only when God stops being faithful and just that He will not forgive and cleanse you, when you sincerely repent of your sins and turn to Him again.

Someone else might say 'You see I knew all these things when I was young and then I used the weapons effectively. I was really hot, but now something has happened and I can't find my way through to victory again.' Stop struggling with your past failures. Look to Jesus by faith. He is the way. Let Him lead you out of your struggles to a state of rest.

Another person may say, 'I just can't understand all you are saying. It is all strange to me.' Then you must repent and be born again, and the Spirit of God will open your understanding to these things.

Conditional

As we go on to examine each of these weapons of war that the Lord has given us, it is good to note the conditions for their effective use. For you to have a clear grasp of what these weapons are and how effective they can be, you have to simply believe the Word of God.

For you to be able to use them effectively you have to meet the following conditions:

Firstly, you must be born again, saved by grace and washed in the precious blood of Jesus Christ.

> *For by grace are ye saved through faith; and that not of yourselves: it is the gift of God: not of works, lest any man should boast.*
>
> (Ephesians 2:8–9)

> *But as many as received him, to them gave he power to become the sons of God, even to them that believe on his name.*
>
> (John 1:12)

You must be living in fellowship with God, having no unconfessed sin in your life. You must be holy and pure, entirely sanctified by the Word of God, and the blood of Jesus Christ.

> *Who shall ascend into the hill of the LORD?*
> *Or who shall stand in his holy place?*
> *He that hath clean hands, and a pure heart;*
> *Who hath not lifted up his soul unto vanity,*
> *Nor sworn deceitfully.*
> *He shall receive the blessing from the LORD,*
> *And righteousness from the God of his*
> *   salvation.*
> *This is the generation of them that seek him,*
> *That seek thy face, O Jacob. Selah.*
>
> (Psalm 24:3–6)

Also, you must accept the lordship of Jesus over your life. He does not have to be your Saviour alone. He is Lord and you must be ready to submit to His lordship in every area of your life.

For none of us liveth to himself, and no man dieth to himself. For whether we live, we live unto the Lord; and whether we die, we die unto the Lord: whether we live therefore, or die, we are the Lord's. For to this end Christ both died, and rose, and revived, that he might be Lord both of the dead and living.

(Romans 14:7–9)

Moreover, you have to walk by faith. Faith is acting on the Word of God. To the person who has chosen to walk by faith, the Word of God becomes so real and so true he does not struggle to believe it, he simply acts on it. At this level, spiritual things become real, as real as your physical body, or your car, or your bed. When you begin to walk by faith it becomes so easy to use the weapons of your warfare effectively.

For we walk by faith, not by sight.

(II Corinthians 5:7)

While we look not at the things which are seen, but at the things which are not seen: for the things which are seen are temporal; but the things which are not seen are eternal.

(II Corinthians 4:18)

Lastly, you must have an unbending desire to be an overcomer in every area of your life. God designs this for you and you should desire no less. Do not be satisfied with anything short of God's best for you in life. Aim at nothing but His perfect will. Having met these conditions you are ready to effectively employ the weapons of our warfare which are not carnal but mighty through God.

Chapter Four

Put On Your Armour

Recently, I was in Lagos for a four-day meeting. Early Sunday morning was free, since my next service would not commence until eleven o'clock. Hence I decided to spend that time at a Full Gospel church whose General Overseer is a friend of our Ministry. It was the concluding service of their organisation's Bible week and he was asked to speak on the subject, 'Militant Soldiers Of Christ'.

'Militant soldiers?' he asked in his opening remark. 'That is a tautology. If you are a soldier you are expected and trained to be militant. You cannot be a soldier and not be militant. Therefore I shall speak on *"Ye are soldiers of Christ"*.' It was a very refreshing service that morning.

Later in the day, it really struck me that although every believer is a soldier of Christ, many don't really live as though they are. When it comes to spiritual warfare they are not militant. God is stirring our hearts at this time, that we may be what we actually are: soldiers of the cross, militant and victorious.

Therefore beloved, as a soldier of Christ, get ready to put on your armour and move into battle.

Finally, my brethren, be strong in the Lord, and in the power of his might. Put on the whole

*armour of God, that ye may be able to stand
against the wiles of the devil. For we wrestle not
against flesh and blood, but against principalities,
against powers, against the rulers of the darkness
of this world, against spiritual wickedness in high
places. Wherefore take unto you the whole armour
of God, that ye may be able to withstand in the evil
day, and having done all, to stand. Stand therefore, having your loins girt about with truth, and
having on the breastplate of righteousness; and
your feet shod with the preparation of the gospel of
peace; above all, taking the shield of faith, wherewith ye shall be able to quench all the fiery darts of
the wicked. And take the helmet of salvation, and
the sword of the Spirit, which is the word of God:
praying always with all prayer and supplication
in the Spirit, and watching thereunto with all
perseverance and supplication for all saints.*

(Ephesians 6:10–18)

Six things are immediately clear from this passage of
Scripture.

First, God wants you to know that you are involved
in spiritual warfare. You are engaged in spiritual battle
against the hierarchy of satanic hosts. This cannot be
over-emphasised.

Second, He wants you to be strong in Him and in the
power of His might. Weakness will do you no good. You
cannot afford to be weak. The weak are to confess that
they are strong, and by so doing turn their weakness
to strength.

Be strong in the Lord. Be strong in the Holy Spirit.
Be strong in the grace that is in Christ Jesus. You are
to be strong and of a good courage. '*Let the weak say,
I am strong*' (Joel 3:10).

Third, God wants you to put on the whole armour He has provided. The armour of God is meant for your complete protection and total victory in spiritual warfare. This has been explained before but is worthy of being repeated.

Moreover, God wants you to stand against, and withstand, the enemy and his devices. He does not want you to be pushed over. He does not want you to be scared, running from the adversary. Rather He wants you to be bold and put the enemy on the run.

Sometime ago, a lady came to me in my office. 'Pastor, please pray for me, the devil is always running after me,' she said. 'Then you must be running in the wrong direction,' I replied. 'The devil is not supposed to be after you. You are to be after the devil. What the Bible says is *"Resist the devil, and he will flee from you."* Stop running,' I counselled her. 'Make a U-turn and begin to give the devil a chase. Through Christ Jesus you are more than a conqueror.'

God wants you to stand in the evil days. There are days when it appears you are losing the battle and odds are against you and everything is going wrong. It appears you are losing control and there seems to be nothing you can do about it. That is the time to refuse to give up and throw in the towel. That is the time to draw strength from the Holy Spirit and still hold on by faith in spite of everything. That is not the time to murmur and complain. That is not the time for a pity party. That is not the time to blame everyone around you. That is not the time to clench your fists at God and complain bitterly at His seeming withdrawal from the scene. Rather, that is the time to stand firm in the faith, giving glory to God, rejoicing in the spirit, expecting the

enemy to flee. That is the right time to sing with
Habakkuk:

Although the fig tree shall not blossom,
Neither shall fruit be in the vines;
The labour of the olive shall fail,
And the fields shall yield no meat;
The flock shall be cut off from the fold,
And there shall be no herd in the stalls:
Yet I will rejoice in the LORD,
I will joy in the God of my salvation.
The LORD God is my strength,
And he will make my feet like hinds' feet,
And he will make me to walk upon mine high
  places.

(Habakkuk 3:17–19)

Beloved, when the evil day comes, you are to stand. And
you shall stand. That was the case with Job. In the evil
day he held on. He refused to give up. The Bible says,
'In all this Job sinned not, nor charged God foolishly'
(Job 1:22).

Having done all, to stand. This is the sixth thing
God wants you to do. Have you just won a battle?
Stand. Have you just made a breakthrough? Stand.
Have you just gone through an evil day and by faith
you have put the enemy on the run? Stand. Have you
just scored a victory for the Kingdom of God? Have you
done exploits in His name? Stand. Soldiers of Christ
are to be ever-ready. The enemy never fights fair. He
strikes at the unguarded hour, when you think you
have every reason to relax.

This means that as a soldier of the cross you are to be
alert at all times. There is no time to put your armour
aside and rest. There is no time to be carried away by a

recent victory and forget that the battle is not yet over.
We are to stand always and fight the good fight of faith,
winning the battle every round in a million. And having
done all, to stand.

The Whole Armour Of God

If you are going to be able to stand in battle, then you
must put on the whole armour of God.

Remember, we are in a battle situation. It is not a
pleasure trip or a game of convenience. The enemy
we fight is so desperate, he wants to do all he can to
defeat us. To be victorious and more than a conqueror,
however, God has ordained that we should fight from
a position of complete safety where the arrows of the
adversary cannot penetrate so that we can be truly
victorious and more than a conqueror. This is the
essence of the armour. It is for total defence such that
'no weapon that is formed against thee shall prosper'
(Isaiah 54:17).

God's plan is that no matter what the enemy has
devised, we should stay on top and be victorious at
all times. Jesus said: *'Behold, I give unto you power
to tread on serpents and scorpions, and over all the
power of the enemy: and nothing shall by any means
hurt you'* (Luke 10:19). Can you see that? While we are
given power to completely devastate all the powers of
the enemy, we are so safe and secure in the armour of
God that *'nothing shall by any means hurt'* us. That is
the perfect will of God.

When we put on the whole armour of God we are
actually dwelling in the secret place of the Most High
under the shadow of the Almighty. There, the enemy
can do nothing. There is no room for any of his tricks

to succeed. We can go on conquering and conquering in the name of the Lord. *'He that dwelleth in the secret place of the most High shall abide under the shadow of the Almighty'* (Psalm 91:1).

While the people of Israel walked in the light of God's Word, no nation on earth could defeat them. When Balak hired Balaam to curse them, the curse would not stick. No attack could succeed. No enchantment or divination could prevail. There was no way the enemy could weaken the people or penetrate their defences. They were putting on the whole armour of God, walking in fellowship with the Almighty and doing His will from the heart. After several fruitless attempts at cursing the people, Balaam cried out in frustration and uttered a most profound prophetic blessing upon the very people he was supposed to curse.

Behold, I have received commandment to bless:
And he hath blessed; and I cannot reverse it.
He hath not beheld iniquity in Jacob,
Neither hath he seen perverseness in Israel:
The LORD his God is with him,
And the shout of a king is among them.
God brought them out of Egypt;
He hath as it were the strength of an unicorn.
Surely there is no enchantment against Jacob,
Neither is there any divination against Israel:
According to this time it shall be said of Jacob
*   and of Israel,*
What hath God wrought!
Behold, the people shall rise up as a great lion,
And lift up himself as a young lion:
He shall not lie down until he eat of the prey,
And drink the blood of the slain.

(Numbers 23:20–24)

Beloved, when you put on the whole armour of God, there is no way the enemy's attacks against you can succeed, whether the attack be spiritual, physical, financial, emotional or through blackmail. You will always be on top and in the place of curses there shall be blessings. There may be occasional setbacks, but your victory is certain in the end.

We need to know, however, that it is the whole armour of God that we must put on and not just some of it, or the parts that take our fancy. That is God's command, not advice. Going into battle without the armour is perilous. Likewise, putting on just some components of the armour is harzardous. This is the reason why a lot of people have become casualties. It is not that God is not strong and mighty enough to save or protect, but when we refuse to put on the whole armour of God we make ourselves vulnerable. This then brings us to a place of discovery of one of the strategies of the enemy. He knows that when we walk with God, under the cover of His whole armour, there is nothing he can do against us. He, therefore, constantly seeks to draw us away from our place of defence, to draw us out of the will of God. At that point, he then strikes. He has succeeded already with too many people. You must not become another victim. Stay under the cover of the whole armour of God. Stay right under the blood of Jesus Christ, the Lamb of God. Stay within God's perfect will for your life.

Remember the children of Israel on the night of the Passover. The angel of destruction visited the whole of Egypt with judgment, and in every house, every first-born son died. But as many Israelites as were under the roof of a house where the blood of the passover lamb had been applied were safe and secure from any harm. They were under a divine cover.

*For I will pass through the land of Egypt this night,
and will smite all the firstborn in the land of Egypt,
both man and beast; and against all the gods of
Egypt I will execute judgment: I am the LORD.
And the blood shall be to you for a token upon the
houses where ye are: and when I see the blood, I
will pass over you, and the plague shall not be
upon you to destroy you, when I smite the land
of Egypt.*

(Exodus 12:12–13)

Rahab, the harlot, and her entire household were safe
from death and destruction when the city of Jericho was
captured and destroyed. How come? They stayed under
the mark of the scarlet thread. There is a covenant
of protection for all who put on the whole armour
of God.

The most striking case in this respect was that of
Daniel. He was an exile in Babylon living in the midst
of a most hostile and jealous people. Because of his
superior wisdom and the divine favour upon his life,
he was promoted above the others by the king. All
governors of the provinces of Babylon were looking
for a way to accuse and destroy him, but they could
not find one.

*Then the presidents and princes sought to find
occasion against Daniel concerning the kingdom;
but they could find none occasion nor fault;
forasmuch as he was faithful, neither was there
any error or fault found in him. Then said these
men, We shall not find any occasion against this
Daniel, except we find it against him concerning
the law of his God.*

(Daniel 6:4–5)

This is it. The man Daniel was completely under the cover of God's armour. He left no loophole for the enemy to take advantage of. Hence they could not get at him. Even when they succeeded in persuading the king to punish him, he could not be touched by the hungry, ravenous lions. There is great power in godliness. Beloved, if you will be impregnable to the enemy, like Daniel, you must put on the whole armour of God.

Having emphasised that God wants us to put on the whole armour He has provided for us, and not just a part of it, we need to know what the components of this armour are and their vital role in our overall protection against the enemy's assault.

Chapter Five

The Whole Armour Of God

I n July 1976, I attended a Christian camp meeting at Iwo, Nigeria. The theme was 'The Whole Armour of God'. The Lord really blessed the meeting. During it we all divided into several smaller groups for a Bible study session. A young lady taught my class and the Lord used her to give me a clear understanding for the first time in my life of what the Bible teaches on 'the whole armour of God'.

There are six components of this armour. Each piece is to be put on with prayer and in faith.

Truth Is An Armour

The first component to be mentioned by Paul in his epistle is truth. *'Stand therefore, having your loins girt about with truth'* (Ephesians 6:14). Why is it the first? I believe it is because of its foremost importance. If you will be victorious in spiritual warfare, if the enemy will not be able to penetrate your defences you must put on truth as an armour. This has a threefold application.

Firstly, Jesus Christ is the truth.

'I am the way, the truth, and the life: no man cometh unto the Father, but by me.'

(John 14:6)

For the law was given by Moses, but grace and truth came by Jesus Christ.

(John 1:17)

From these verses of Scripture, it is clear that all truth is in Christ. When you know Jesus, you know the truth. When you receive Him as your Saviour and Lord you are putting on the truth. It is essential you do so if you have not already, for there can be neither victory nor safety without Him. However, after knowing Jesus as our Lord and Saviour, we need to relate to, and fellowship with Him daily as we study His Word. This will help us to be victorious over sin and temptation. The Bible makes it clear that there is always a struggle between the flesh and the spirit. The flesh wants to drag us into sin so we can displease God and dishonour His name.

For the flesh lusteth against the Spirit, and the Spirit against the flesh: and these are contrary the one to the other: so that ye cannot do the things that ye would.

(Galatians 5:17)

Remember, lying is of the devil. Jesus told the Pharisees and Sadducees:

Ye are of your father the devil, and the lusts of your father ye will do. He was a murderer from the beginning, and abode not in the truth, because there is no truth in him. When he speaketh a lie, he speaketh of his own: for he is a liar, and the father of it.

(John 8:44)

Lying, therefore, projects you as a child of the devil. If
you are born again you have nothing to do with lying.
Be like God your Father. Be like Jesus your Saviour.
Put on the armour of truth and let it reflect in all the
things you say or do. Give no room for lying, for no liar
shall enter the Kingdom of God.

Some people are under the influence of a lying spirit.
They just cannot help but lie. Such people need to
decisively claim their victory through the blood of Jesus
and make up their minds not to lie again. It will help
to find a minister of deliverance to minister to you if
you are in that situation. You need to be free.

Nothing matters in life like integrity. If we are going
to win the battle of life we must renounce all the hidden
things of dishonesty and live a life of integrity. Paul the
apostle said this about himself:

> *Therefore seeing we have this ministry, as we*
> *have received mercy, we faint not; but have*
> *renounced the hidden things of dishonesty, not*
> *walking in craftiness, nor handling the word of*
> *God deceitfully; but by manifestation of the truth*
> *commending ourselves to every man's conscience*
> *in the sight of God.*
>
> (II Corinthians 4:1–2)

When you walk in the truth, you commend yourself to
every man's conscience. People trust and respect you.
You are putting on the whole armour of God and it
will protect you in the days of calamity. Integrity will
give you a good name, and a good name is to be chosen
rather than silver and gold.

I cannot forget an experience I had with the Lord in
1980, shortly before I entered into the ministry full-
time. I was conducting a survey in Ogun State – I was

a land surveyor. I was behind my theodolite and trying to get a straight line when I heard the Lord speak very clearly to me, '**Son, do you want to go far with me? Do you want my blessing upon your ministry and services for me? Then be sincere with yourself, with others, and with me.**' That was a ministration that changed my life entirely. I saw clearly how God hates hypocrisy and desires truth in the inward part.

Be sincere. Be a man of truth. A man of integrity. A man of sincerity. That makes you enjoy your relationship with God on a daily basis. Lies of any kind must never come out of your mouth. You must be a man or woman of integrity. Integrity will preserve you.

Righteousness As An Armour

. . . and having on the breastplate of righteousness.
(Ephesians 6:14)

Righteousness is your breastplate. Beloved, put it on. As the breastplate, it covers the most vital part of the body – the heart. If for any reason the heart is exposed and the enemy's arrow is allowed to penetrate, the result is death. That is why you must never take lightly this component of God's armour – righteousness. Righteousness has been described as 'right standing with God' or the ability to stand before God without any sense of sin, or guilt or shame. This is vital. It implies that without righteousness, there can be no fellowship with the Father, nor answer to prayers, nor victory in spiritual warfare. But with righteousness everything is all right.

The Bible makes it clear that Jesus is our righteousness. He has been made for us '*wisdom, and righteousness, and sanctification, and redemption'* (I Corinthians 1:30). Without Jesus Christ, there is no way a man can have access to the Father, nor be able to stand before Him, or enjoy fellowship with Him. Without His precious blood that He shed on the cross at Calvary there is no way we can enjoy the forgiveness of our sins or be free from guilt and condemnation.

But when Jesus Christ offered Himself as our ransom on the cross, He became our righteousness. By putting our faith in Him we become the righteousness of God. The Bible says,

> *For he hath made him to be sin for us, who knew no sin; that we might be made the righteousness of God in him.*
>
> (II Corinthians 5:21)

Because He has made righteousness available to us we can be forgiven our past sins and be free indeed.

> *There is therefore now no condemnation to them which are in Christ Jesus, who walk not after the flesh, but after the Spirit.*
>
> (Romans 8:1)

He made righteousness available to us, we can be washed and cleansed from the filth of sin and become holy and unblameable in Christ. That is what His blood does. It purges our conscience from dead works to serve the living God. It so purifies our heart and entire being, leaving no stain of sin, that we stand before God as though we had never sinned before.

> *For if the blood of bulls and of goats, and the ashes of an heifer sprinkling the unclean, sanctifieth*

to the purifying of the flesh: how much more shall the blood of Christ, who through the eternal Spirit offered himself without spot to God, purge your conscience from dead works to serve the living God?

(Hebrews 9:13–14)

The blood of Jesus Christ his Son cleanseth us from all sin.

(I John 1:7)

That is why it is so ridiculous for someone to think of being righteous without Jesus Christ. Some folks think that because they are religious, or morally straight, then they are righteous. Never. That is nothing but self-righteousness which is like filthy rags before the Lord:

But we are all as an unclean thing, and all our righteousnesses are as filthy rags; and we all do fade as a leaf; and our iniquities, like the wind, have taken us away.

(Isaiah 64:6)

Apostle Paul belonged to this category before he was born again. He was very religious. He boasted in being a direct descendant of Abraham. He was religiously zealous. And he was very sincere in all he did. Nevertheless he was wrong. But after he met Jesus, the story changed. He knew then what true righteousness means, and that it can be attained only by faith in Christ Jesus. This is his testimony:

For we are the circumcision, which worship God in the spirit, and rejoice in Christ Jesus, and have no confidence in the flesh.
Though I might also have confidence in the

flesh. If any other man thinketh that he hath whereof he might trust in the flesh, I more: circumcised the eighth day, of the stock of Israel, of the tribe of Benjamin, an Hebrew of the Hebrews; as touching the law, a Pharisee; concerning zeal, persecuting the church; touching the righteousness which is in the law, blameless.

But what things were gain to me, those I counted loss for Christ. Yea doubtless, and I count all things but loss for the excellency of the knowledge of Christ Jesus my Lord: for whom I have suffered the loss of all things, and do count them but dung, that I may win Christ, and be found in him, not having mine own righteousness, which is of the law, but that which is through the faith of Christ, the righteousness which is of God by faith: that I may know him, and the power of his resurrection, and the fellowship of his sufferings, being made conformable unto his death.

(Philippians 3:3–10)

The message is clear. True righteousness comes by faith in Christ Jesus. And that is what you are to put on.

When you put on the breastplate of righteousness the fruit will show. That is what the Bible calls the fruit of righteousness. It is the same as the fruit of the Spirit. When a man is righteous he will live righteously. There are folks who claim that they are the righteousness of God in Christ Jesus yet live so shamefully. They are immoral. They lack integrity. Their financial dealings are shady. They do not pay their debts. Neither do they honour their pledges and obligations. They rarely keep their promises. And they know no shame. Such

people should be told that they need to bring forth
the fruit of righteousness. John, the beloved, put it
simply:

> *Little children, let no man deceive you: he that
> doeth righteousness is righteous, even as he is
> righteous. He that committeth sin is of the devil;
> for the devil sinneth from the beginning. For this
> purpose the Son of God was manifested, that he
> might destroy the works of the devil.*
>
> (I John 3:7–8)

The message is very clear. If a man thinks he is
righteous but is not walking in righteousness, and is
living in sin, he is deceived. The man that is righteous
is like Jesus. He lives righteously as a daily practice.
*'He that saith he abideth in him ought himself also so
to walk, even as he walked'* (I John 2:6)

Therefore, beloved, put on your breastplate of righteousness. Stand right before the Lord without guilt or
condemnation, having been washed by the precious
blood of Jesus. Stand before the watching world as
evidence of the true righteousness of God that comes
by faith in Christ Jesus.

The Gospel Is The Power Of God

> *And your feet shod with the preparation of the
> gospel of peace.*
>
> (Ephesians 6:15)

Your readiness to preach the Gospel is part of your
armour as a soldier of the cross. We are to preach the
Gospel *'in season, out of season'* (II Timothy 4:2).

We are not to keep quiet but to boldly declare the whole counsel of God. This is a major way of fighting the good fight of faith and we all are to be involved in it.

The last charge that our Lord Jesus gave us before He left the world was for us to go into all the world and preach the Gospel to every creature. This is what Bible scholars call the Great Commission:

> *And Jesus came and spake unto them, saying, All power is given unto me in heaven and in earth. Go ye therefore, and teach all nations, baptizing them in the name of the Father, and of the Son, and of the Holy Ghost: teaching them to observe all things whatsoever I have commanded you: and, lo, I am with you alway, even unto the end of the world. Amen.*

> (Matthew 28:18–20)

Your obedience to the Great Commission is part of your armour against the wiles of the devil. I have come to realise that the reason why a lot of Christians are weak and spiritually anaemic is that they are not playing any active role in the Great Commission. They are not involved in praying, in giving, in witnessing, in going. They just don't care. There is nothing that terrifies the devil as much as a Christian being actively involved in evangelism and mission. Jesus our Lord said,

> *Behold, I give unto you power to tread on serpents and scorpions, and over all the power of the enemy: and nothing shall by any means hurt you.*

> (Luke 10:19)

Treading on serpents and scorpions and over all the powers of the enemy! How do you tread on them all? Of

course, it is with your sandals or shoes. What consti-
tutes these? *'And your feet shod with the preparation
of the gospel of peace'* (Ephesians 6:15).

Again the Bible clearly states that our victory over
the devil comes by the blood of the Lamb and Word of
our testimony. What is the Word of our testimony. It
is the Gospel that we preach. This Gospel is the power
of God for the salvation of whoever believes. Therefore,
beloved, put on this armour today. Begin to preach the
Gospel of Jesus more fervently than ever before. Not
only will you win the battle of life, you will be a terror
to the devil.

The Shield Of Faith

*Above all, taking the shield of faith, wherewith
ye shall be able to quench all the fiery darts of the
wicked.*

(Ephesians 6:16)

Your shield of faith is a crucial component of God's
armour. This is why the Bible urges us to take the
shield of faith, 'above all'. Without it, defeat is inevitable because the battle we are fighting is 'the good
fight of faith'. We fight by faith; we win by faith.

Faith is what will turn to nothing the fiery darts
of the wicked. You can be sure the enemy will throw
those darts at you: temptations, fear, discouragement,
apparent lack, oppositions, persecutions, and all manner of demonic attacks. They are the fiery darts of the
wicked. As you hold your shield of faith, you are not
affected by any of them. You move ahead by faith to
triumph against the enemy in spite of his fiery darts.

There is a statement that occurs about four times in the Scriptures:

But the just shall live by his faith.

(Habakkuk 2:4b)

The just shall live by faith.

(Romans 1:17)

For, the just shall live by faith.

(Galatians 3:11)

Now the just shall live by faith: But if any man draw back, my soul shall have no pleasure in him.

(Hebrews 10:38)

These statements are not written in Scripture just to fill up space. God has decided to repeat this same fact over and over because it is crucial to our victory in spiritual warfare. The man who will live at all must live by his faith. There is a difference between living and merely existing. 'The just shall live by faith.' All of God's blessings are received by faith.

Salvation: *'For by grace are ye saved through faith'.*

(Ephesians 2:8)

Healing: *'Thy faith hath made thee whole.'*

(Mark 5:34)

Baptism in the Holy Spirit: *'He therefore that ministereth to you the Spirit, and worketh miracles among you, doeth he it by the works of the law, or by the hearing of faith?'* (Galatians 3:5).

The answer is obvious. No matter what blessing a man wants from God, he must come by faith, otherwise he will receive nothing. The Bible makes it clear that even to please the Lord we must live by faith.

But without faith it is impossible to please him:
for he that cometh to God must believe that he is,
and that he is a rewarder of them that diligently
seek him.

                                                    (Hebrews 11:6)

It is by faith we please God. It is by faith we overcome
the adversary. It is by faith we overcome temptations.
It is by faith we inherit and enjoy the promise of God.

Smith Wigglesworth, the renowned British preacher
of old, once said, 'I am not moved by what I see, I am
not moved by what I feel, I am not moved by what I
hear. I am only moved by the Word of God.' That is
what it means to live by faith. *'For we walk by faith,*
and not by sight' (II Corinthians 5:7).

You are encouraged beloved, *'not to be slothful, but*
to be followers of them who through faith and patience
inherit the promises' (Hebrews 6:12). Hold up your
shield of faith, and you are sure to win in spiritual
warfare.

The Helmet Of Salvation

There is nothing the enemy aims at like the head. In
warfare situations the head is a prime target for the
adversary. The moment the head is gone the battle is
over. That is why it is crucial that our head should be
covered by the helmet of God's salvation.

There are a lot of people in church trying to fight
spiritual warfare who are neither sure of their salvation
nor have a definite testimony of conversion to Christ.
Many of these equate religious activities with salvation.
Others hang upon parental connections. Because they
are born of Christian parents, they reason, they must be

Christians. Nothing can be further from the truth! The fact is that Christianity is an individual experience of personal relationship with Jesus, as Lord and Saviour. Jesus Christ said, *'Except a man be born again, he cannot see the kingdom of God'* (John 3:3).

This experience of the new birth is *'not of blood, nor of the will of the flesh, nor of the will of man, but of God'* (John 1:13). If you have not been born again, you are like a soldier going into enemy territory without any cover for his head. He will soon be blown to pieces.

There are others who practise a mixture of Christian convictions and other things. Some mix it up with the practice of witchcraft. There are many in Africa who mix the Christian faith with traditional religions. Many mix it up with occult practices, freemasonary and other secret societies. Some others mix it up with metaphysics, transcendental meditation and other Eastern occult practices and religions. This is part of the plot of Satan to rob people of their helmet of salvation. Jesus will not entertain any bargaining. You either belong to Him altogether or you do not belong to Him at all. What the Bible says is that you shall love the Lord your God with *'all thy heart, and with all thy soul, and with all thy mind'* (Matthew 22:37). It is all or nothing. You cannot serve two masters.

That is why it is important for you to make a clear choice of whom you will serve. I made my choice several years ago. There is no room for giving the devil any foothold. Whether in life or in death, under whatever circumstances, Jesus Christ is the Lord over my entire being. You also must make your choice today if you have not already. Don't let the devil fool you; you cannot serve God and mammon. The words of Joshua to the people of Israel, shortly before he died, are appropriate at this juncture.

Now therefore fear the LORD, and serve him in sincerity and in truth: and put away the gods which your fathers served on the other side of the flood, and in Egypt; and serve ye the LORD. And if it seem evil unto you to serve the LORD, choose you this day whom ye will serve; whether the gods which your fathers served that were on the other side of the flood, or the gods of the Amorites, in whose land ye dwell: but as for me and my house, we will serve the LORD.

(Joshua 24:14–75)

So, the helmet of salvation is a vital element in God's armour, and it is free. Jesus has paid the price with His blood to purchase our salvation. All we need to do is to receive it by faith. It is the gift of God and it is available for all – young, old, male, female, rich or poor.

For the wages of sin is death; but the gift of God is eternal life through Jesus Christ our Lord.

(Romans 6:23)

For by grace are ye saved through faith; and that not of yourselves: it is the gift of God: not of works, lest any man should boast.

(Ephesians 2:8–9)

The Sword Of The Spirit

And take . . . the sword of the Spirit, which is the word of God.

(Ephesians 6:17)

This is both an offensive and defensive weapon. It is a most crucial element of God's armour for us. God has ordained that we should live by His Word, fight and win our battles with His Word.

It was that same Word that Jesus Christ used to defeat the adversary: *'It is written.'* And that silenced the enemy forever. The same Word is available to us and we can use it to deal with Satan effectively.

This Word is the lamp to our feet and light to our path. To neglect the Word is to walk in darkness. We are in the age when God is pouring out His Spirit upon all flesh. Coming along with this outpouring is the abundant revelation knowledge of the Word of God. We now have much teaching available to us. Yet it does no good until, as an individual, you take advantage of what God has given you, and diligently apply the Word of God in your life.

A whole chapter in this book is devoted to the place of the Word in spiritual battle. It is, however, vital to mention here that it is the Christian that gives priority attention to the Word of God who will become what God actually wants him to be. He also will be able to put the enemy where he properly belongs.

Therefore, make time for the Word; promote it and it shall promote you. Love it and your victory is certain.

The Vital Place Of Prayer

Each element of God's armour is to be put on with prayer. It is prevailing prayer that really makes it work. And we are to pray with all manner of prayer and supplication, praying with the spirit and praying with the understanding also.

> *For if I pray in an unknown tongue, my spirit prayeth, but my understanding is unfruitful. What*

is it then? I will pray with the spirit, and I will
pray with the understanding also: I will sing with
the spirit, and I will sing with the understand-
ing also.

(I Corinthians 14:14–15)

As we do this we find that we are totally secure and our
complete protection is guaranteed. We can then fight
the adversary from a position of complete safety.

Praying always with all prayer and supplication
in the Spirit, and watching thereunto with all
perseverance and supplication for all saints.

(Ephesians 6:18)

Applying the armour of God with fervent prayer
makes you invincible. The enemy cannot penetrate
your defences. Prayer also makes you successful in
every endeavour of your life. There is a spiritual
equation I learnt some years ago. With the benefit
of hindsight I know this equation works with math-
ematical precision:

No prayer   – no success
Little prayer – little success
Much prayer – much success

We should not wonder, then how saints of God like
Moses, Joshua, Samuel, David, Peter and Paul made
such a success of their spiritual lives. They gave themselves to much prayer. We should not wonder why
Jesus was so successful in accomplishing the will of
the Father within such a short three and a half years
of ministry – a brief life on earth that has had an
unparalleled effect. He gave Himself to prayer. Much

prayer. Fervent prayer. Prevailing prayer. If we also will do the same, we will doubtless make a glorious success of the Father's will for our lives. I urge you then to determine to do what the early disciples did as expressed in the Book of Acts. *'But we will give ourselves continually to prayer, and to the ministry of the word'* (Acts 6:4).

Chapter Six

The Name Of Jesus

That at the name of Jesus every knee should bow . . .

(Philippians 2:10)

T he name of Jesus is a mighty weapon God has provided for us to fight a good warfare. It is very effective and unfailing when applied. It works great wonders when it is rightly used. As children of God, made righteous in the blood of Jesus, the name serves as a strong refuge as well.

The name of the LORD is a strong tower:
The righteous runneth into it, and is safe.

(Proverbs 18:10)

The Worth Of The Name

The worth of a name depends on the amount of authority the bearer of it has, or the degree of influence he can exert. For instance someone who has a million dollars deposited in a bank is capable of issuing a cheque covering one thousand dollars in his name and it shall be honoured. As far as that bank is concerned he has financial authority up to a million dollars. Supposing another man has a thousand people working under him, any instruction in his name to any of those workers shall be promptly obeyed.

What is the name of Jesus worth? It is worth the whole universe – and more. He created the whole universe – He is Lord over it, and all things are subject to Him. *'All things were made by him; and without him was not anything made that was made'* (John 1:3).

All things – whether physical or spiritual; visible or invisible; demons, angels, men. All things were made by Him and for Him. So they are subject to His name.

For by him were all things created, that are in heaven, and that are in earth, visible and invisible, whether they be thrones, or dominions, or principalities, or powers: all things were created by him and for him.

(Colossians 1:16)

It is just simply logical that all things are subject to His name because He created all things.

He Redeemed All Things

He has authority over all things, because He has redeemed all things by His precious blood.

Man was created in the image of God to have dominion over the earth and all other works of God (Genesis 1:26–28; Psalm 8:5–6). But man sold out to the devil, the enemy, thereby bringing the whole creation under the curse of God and under the dominion of the devil. Then Jesus came and paid the price and legally redeemed all things back to God. *'For to this end Christ both died, and rose, and revived, that he might be Lord both of the dead and living'* (Romans 14:9).

Because He has conquered all the enemies that are against us, He is Lord of all. Jesus met the devil and defeated him in the wilderness, in Gethsemane, on the cross and in hell, and He arose triumphantly, the victorious Lord.

He has conquered all the demons, principalities and powers that contend against us. The Bible says He 'spoiled' them all.

As well as conquering the devil who had the power of death, He also conquered death (Hebrews 2:14–15). He conquered the grave. He destroyed all weapons used by the enemy to hold us in bondage. Therefore, by using His name we can enforce the victory He has wrought. Satan and his demons must respond to Jesus' name because they know that He has conquered them all.

> *Blotting out the handwriting of ordinances that was against us, which was contrary to us, and took it out of the way, nailing it to his cross; and having spoiled principalities and powers, he made a shew of them openly, triumphing over them in it.*
>
> (Colossians 2:14–15)

> *Forasmuch then as the children are partakers of flesh and blood, he also himself likewise took part of the same; that through death he might destroy him that had the power of death, that is, the devil; and deliver them who through fear of death were all their lifetime subject to bondage.*
>
> (Hebrews 2:14–15)

The Supreme Name

After Jesus had finished the work of our redemption,
the Father bestowed on Him the supreme name of all
in the universe. At this name, every knee must bow and
every tongue confess that He is Lord. This is clearly
stated in the Word of God.

> *Wherefore [as a result of what he has done] God
> also hath highly exalted him, and given him a
> name which is above every name: that at the
> name of Jesus every knee should bow, of things
> in heaven, and things in earth, and things under
> the earth; and that every tongue should confess
> that Jesus Christ is Lord, to the glory of God the
> Father.*
>
> (Philippians 2:9–11)

Think about it. God Himself bestowed this name on
Jesus. This name is above every other name. The
mention of this name commands the obeisance of all
things, on earth, in heaven and in hell. The name is
supreme and therefore, everyone should call Him Lord.
Jesus is occupying a place of supreme authority in the
whole universe, hence His name is highly authoritative.
Scripture talks of this supreme position of Jesus both
now and for all eternity.

> *[God] raised him from the dead, and set him at
> his own right hand in the heavenly places, far
> above all principality, and power, and might,
> and dominion, and every name that is named,
> not only in this world, but also in that which is
> to come.*
>
> (Ephesians 1:20–21)

The name of Jesus is above all names and when it is spoken in faith it works effectively, healing sicknesses, sending out demons, bringing God-sent victory and deliverance in all situations. The Father Himself has ordained that *'in all things he [Jesus] might have the preeminence'* (Colossians 1:18).

As you speak that name, say it with reverence, confidence and boldness and you will be surprised to see how it works. The name of Jesus must be honoured in heaven, on earth and under the earth.

The Devil Trembles At His Name

The name of Jesus represents all that He has done and all that He is. The devil himself recognises the supremacy of the name of Jesus and he trembles. The best way of dealing with him is by using Jesus' name.

> *And when he was come to the other side into the country of the Gergesenes, there met him two possessed with devils, coming out of the tombs, exceeding fierce, . . . And, behold, they cried out, saying, What have we to do with thee, Jesus, thou Son of God? art thou come hither to torment us before the time?*
>
> (Matthew 8:28–29)

Do you see how demons tremble in His presence? What is true of His person is true of His name today, when used in faith.

At another time when Paul was using the name of Jesus to deal with the devil, the demons confessed the supremacy of that name. Sometime later, a demon said *'Jesus I know, and Paul I know'* (Acts 19:15). This also

shows that they recognise the authority of a servant
of God using the name of Jesus, and they must therefore bow. Still today that name makes everybody and
everything bow when it is spoken in faith.

A brother once shared a testimony about his past
membership of many secret societies. They practised
astral projection and out-of-the-body experiences as
part of their occult rituals. One day they were having
one of their secret out-of-the-body-projection meetings
in the spiritual realm by the Bar-beach in Lagos. A man
came around and unknowingly stepped in their midst
and began to pray. (As they were operating in the spiritual realm and in the dark the man did not see them.)

These men of the underworld felt slighted and decided
to strangle this man to death. Immediately they held
him, he shouted the name of Jesus. This brother (now
an evangelist for Jesus) said that they suddenly saw
flaming swords which proceeded from various directions
and scattered them. That put an end to their meeting that
day. The name of Jesus is above all demons and powers of
darkness. Witches, wizards, familiar spirits and all evil
must bow to the name – the name above all names.

The Name Is For Us

The name of Jesus is for us. All that He did was done
for us. The conquest He made and the victories that
He won were all for us. And the Father has given us
the name to use boldly and authoritatively in fighting
against the devil. The name is for us. The Bible says
that God has given Jesus for the Church to have
authority over all things.

And he [God] has put all things under his [Jesus']
feet and has made him [Jesus] the head over all

> *things for the church, which is his body, the*
> *fulness of him who fills all in all.*
>   (Ephesians 1:22–23 RSV)

If you have been born again, His name is for you. You
can begin to use the name boldly from today and you
shall know true victory. The Lord Jesus conferred upon
every believer in Him tremendous spiritual authority
when He told us to freely use His name in spiritual
battles. *'In my name . . .'*, means we can use His
name to accomplish what He could have done were
He to be physically present today. The name is not
only meant for some super-Christians; but everyone
who truly believes in Christ as his Saviour and Lord.

Salvation Is In That Name Alone

The salvation of any human being lies in the name of
Jesus. He alone bled and died for our sins and in Him
alone is the hope of eternal life. *'In him was life; and
the life was the light of men'* (John 1:4).

The angel that announced the birth of the Lord Jesus
said: *'Thou shalt call his name JESUS: for he shall save
his people from their sins'* (Matthew 1:21). It is useless
and hopeless trusting in anything else for salvation.
Salvation is not found in any religious establishment
or organisation. Salvation is not in rituals, ceremonies,
clothes – the carnal ordinances of men. Salvation is in
one name. Not just any name, but the name of Jesus.

> *Neither is there salvation in any other: for there is*
> *none other name under heaven given among men,*
> *whereby we must be saved.*
>
>   (Acts 4:12)

Have you been saved from sin, and the coming judgment? Are you born again? The name of Jesus gives you complete salvation from sin, Satan and all his works. You can trust in that name and be saved for evermore.

Repent, and be baptized every one of you in the name of Jesus Christ for the remission of sins, and ye shall receive the gift of the Holy Ghost.

(Acts 2:38)

Using The Name In Conflicts

The devil is the source of all the problems, conflicts and temptations the Christian meets in life. We should know this and know also that the sure way to win is by using the name of Jesus.

One night I was travelling in a commercial vehicle, moving at high speed. Suddenly, we came across a trailer that had turned over across our side of the road. The driver was very close before he saw it and there seemed to be no way out, as we swerved and saw another vehicle blocking that part of the road leaving just a narrow gap between. We were going to crash. I shouted 'Jesus' – that was the only thing I could do. But it worked a miracle. How the vehicle managed to get through that narrow space still remains a mystery. The devil planned untimely death for me and the other passengers, but all escaped through the use of the name of Jesus. There are countless testimonies of how children of God have used the name of Jesus to overcome the enemy in their various situations.

In temptations, in crises, when things are hard, let us use the name of Jesus. Uttering that name by faith releases a tremendous spiritual force that defeats the devil.

We cannot use any carnal weapon to overcome the devil. Reasoning? Philosophising? Arguing? The devil has used all these to defeat people thousands of years back, and he is still doing so today. He's quite experienced at it. If you seek to match strength with Satan you are surely going to fail. But the devil has no trick to use against the name of Jesus. Whether it is a temptation, a difficulty, a sickness, a demonic attack against you or a loved one, use the name of Jesus. Your victory is sure.

> *Some trust in chariots, and some in horses:*
> *But we will remember the name of the LORD*
> * our God.*
> *They are brought down and fallen:*
> *But we are risen, and stand upright.*
>
> (Psalm 20:7–8)

Using The Name In Prayer

The name of Jesus is the key that unlocks the treasure house of God. We use it to enter and have as much grace, strength, blessing as we need, both for ourselves and for others.

Jesus taught us not to pray to Him but to ask the Father for whatever we want in His name and that we shall receive it. That we have not always followed this rule has been the reason for many unanswered prayers.

*And in that day ye shall ask me nothing. Verily,
verily, I say unto you, Whatsoever ye shall ask the
Father in my name, he will give it you.*

(John 16:23)

We have the great privilege of using the name of Jesus
in prayer. It is a guarantee that we shall have our
petitions answered, when they are in the will of God.
He is taking our place at the right hand of the Father
both to intercede for us, and to ensure that the answers
to our petitions are not hindered. We are His body,
taking His place on earth, doing His work and using
His name to get things done. The more boldly we use
His name the greater results we get and the greater
glory we bring to the Father. The apostles knew the
secret of using His name and they used it with great
boldness and got great results.

Healing And Miracles In The Name

It is in the name alone that wonders and miracles are
wrought. Many people say that the age of miracles is
past, that it ceased with the apostles of Christ. This is
utter nonsense. There is the God of miracles, working
miracles and wonders in all ages. He has not changed.
'For I am the LORD, I change not . . .' (Malachi 3:6).
The same Jesus who worked miracles when He was
physically on earth is alive today. He is still present
on earth by His Spirit, working miracles through His
disciples. *'Jesus Christ the same yesterday, and today,
and forever'* (Hebrews 13:8).

Jesus gave us a fantastic promise that we shall work
miracles in His name.

*Verily, verily, I say unto you, He that believeth
on me, the works that I do shall he do also; and
greater works than these shall he do; because I go
unto my Father.*

(John 14:12)

This is a great challenge. We can do the work that He
did – even greater works. What were the works that He
was doing? Was He praying? Yes He prayed, but that
was to enable Him to do the works the Father sent Him
to do.

*God anointed Jesus of Nazareth with the Holy
Ghost and with power: who went about doing
good, and healing all that were oppressed of the
devil, for God was with him.*

(Acts 10:38)

These and greater works He told us that we will do if
we believe Him for them – healing the sick, casting
out devils, delivering all that are being oppressed of
the devil, turning people back to God.

The Lord told us we can do these works by demanding, and by commanding them to be, in His name. And
when we demand such things in His name, He said He
shall ensure that it is done. And when it is done, the
Father is glorified in the Son.

*And whatsoever ye shall ask [or demand or com-
mand to be] in my name, that will I do, that the
Father may be glorified in the Son. If ye shall ask
[demand, command to be] anything in my name,
I will do it.'*

(John 14:13–14)

We get a clear picture of this in the life of Peter and John. One day they were going to the temple to worship. At the gate was a lame man begging for alms. He was hoping for some coins from Peter and John. They had none; but they had the name of Jesus. By using His name they demanded a miracle; they commanded into being the healing of this man.

> *Then Peter said, Silver and gold have I none; but such as I have give I thee: In the name of Jesus Christ of Nazareth rise up and walk.*
>
> (Acts 3:6)

And it was so. The Lord Jesus did it and so the Father was glorified in the Son. The man was pulled up, and '*walking and leaping*' he began to praise the Lord.

When Peter and John were called to question by the religious leaders as to how the miracle was performed, they answered:

> *And his name through faith in his name hath made this man strong, whom ye see and know: yea, the faith which is by him hath given him this perfect soundness in the presence of you all.*
>
> (Acts 3:16)

Killing The Giants In Your Life

We are all familiar with the story of how David killed Goliath. Goliath was a giant, an intimidator. For a long time he had terrorised the army of Israel and no one dared challenge him. The description the Bible gives of this man explains why. A soldier from his youth, taller and bigger than any man around, fully armed, carrying such unusually large weapons, the Israelites simply did not know what to do with him. They were all stricken with fear, including King Saul, the man who was supposed to lead them to battle.

Then came David, a young 'boy' who had never had any military experience or training. Seeing and hearing Goliath humiliating the army of Israel, stirred him up and he decided to fight him in the name of the Lord God of hosts.

Humanly, it was a battle of unequals, Goliath being fully armed, heavily demonised and big out of all proportion; David, a simple shepherd boy with just a sling and five stones.

As Goliath drew near David in battle, the Bible says, *'the Philistine looked about, and saw David, he disdained him . . . And . . . cursed David by his gods'* (I Samuel 17:42–43).

That certainly brought a spiritual dimension to the battle. Goliath was fighting by his gods, releasing terrible demonic forces against David. How did David respond?

Then said David to the Philistine, Thou comest to me with a sword, and with a spear, and with a shield: but I come to thee in the name of the LORD of hosts, the God of the armies of Israel, whom thous hast defied. This day will the LORD deliver thee into mine hand; and I will smite thee, and take thine head from thee; and I will give the carcases of the host of the Philistines this day unto the fowls of the air, and to the wild beasts of the earth; that all the earth may know that there is a God in Israel. And all this assembly shall know that the LORD saveth not with sword and spear: for

> *the battle is the LORD's, and he will give you into*
> *our hands.*
>
> (I Samuel 17:45—47)

David confronted Goliath in the name of the Lord. Was he disappointed? Never. There can be no disappointment when we trust in the name of the Lord.

The name of Jesus never fails. David killed the giant and cut off his head. Therefore, beloved, confront that giant in your life with this triumphant name. It does not really matter what the giant may be. The name of Jesus will conquer whatever giant you may meet in life and give you victory. Do not let that giant continue to terrorise and intimidate you. Commit whatever it is today to the name of the Lord and your victory is certain.

This is what the Lord wants every Christian to believe Him for. Note that He said *'He that believeth on me, the works that I do shall he do also; and greater works . . .'*. This promise is for anybody who has enough faith. To further prove that it is meant for every Christian, the Lord said, while commanding us to preach the Gospel to every creature, that we should use His name to work miracles and healings.

> *Go ye into all the world, and preach the gospel to*
> *every creature. He that believeth and is baptized*
> *shall be saved; but he that believeth not shall be*
> *damned. And these signs shall follow them that*
> *believe; In my name shall they cast out devils;*
> *they shall speak with new tongues; they shall take*
> *up serpents; and if they drink any deadly thing, it*
> *shall not hurt them; they shall lay hands on the*
> *sick, and they shall recover.*
>
> (Mark 16:15—18)

The early disciples knew and understood the authority that is invested in the name of Jesus, and they took advantage of it. They used it effectively and it worked for them. We believe firmly that the Lord is raising a people in these last days in our land who shall be fully conscious of who and what they are in Christ, and what great weapons of war the Lord has provided for them. They shall walk in this consciousness and march through the length and breadth of this land like flames of fire, enforcing the victory of Calvary on the enemy. They shall carry the full Gospel message far and wide through the power of the resurrected Christ and His great name.

Abiding In The Realm Of Victory

It is in the name of the Lord Jesus that we are saved. When we gather together we gather in His name (Matthew 18:20). We are baptised in His name (Matthew 28:19; Acts 2:38). The way to victory in the Christian life is in His name.

How do we abide in the realm of victory? This is a question that bothers many Christians. It is those who have actually experienced many defeats that can appreciate how precious this question is. The answer is simple and if we take the Word of God as it is and act on it, we shall abide in the realm of victory.

And whatsoever ye do in word or deed, do all in the name of the Lord Jesus, giving thanks to God and the Father by him.

(Colossians 3:17)

That is it. Doing all things in the name of Jesus, and giving thanks to God through Him in the process.

Can you begin to practise it in the strength of the
Lord? Eating, sleeping, having a discussion, working,
travelling, reading, buying, writing, waking, bathing
etc. – do everything in the name of this Jesus and give
thanks. There is no one who, doing this, will not live a
victorious life.

First, it will keep the devil off your track because the
name of Jesus will make him flee from you.

Secondly, it will destroy every form of satanic influence existing in whatever you lay your hands on.

Thirdly, it will keep you from worrying, and keep you
at peace. You are guaranteed that all is well because
you do all things in the name of Jesus. This is living
in the realm of victory.

Lastly, it turns your seeming defeats into victory and
your mistakes to blessings. As you act in the name of
Jesus, the Lord knows how to use even your mistakes
and failures to glorify His name and bring shame to the
enemy. Remember, He makes all things work together
for good for them that love Him (Romans 8:28).

Sometime ago, during a meeting, the Spirit of the
Lord inspired me to give these words of prophecy on
the name of Jesus.

The knowledge of His glory shall yet increase, for
it has pleased the Father to give Him preeminence
in all things.

The knowledge of His victory shall yet increase,
for wherever the story of the cross is told, the
victory of the resurrection must be made manifest.
And behold the name – the name of Jesus . . . It is
given to you for success.

It is given to you for victory.

It is given to you for glory.

And if you will lay hold of what has been given to you, and train your tongue to maintain a positive confession, you shall abide in the realm of victory.

Arise then and lay hold of the name of Jesus. Use it boldly in all things and you shall abide in the realm of victory.

Chapter Seven

The Blood Of The Lamb

Jesus is the Lamb of God that was slain for our sins. When John the Baptist saw Him, he exclaimed, *'Behold the Lamb of God, which taketh away the sin of the world'* (John 1:29).

It is His blood that was shed on Calvary for our sins, to purge us so that we might be holy and blameless before God, and thereby have eternal life.

Man is a rebel. Everyone is a sinner. *'All we like sheep have gone astray'* (Isaiah 53:6). But Jesus shed His blood to bring us back to God. The Bible says, *'But now in Christ Jesus ye who sometimes were far off are made nigh by the blood of Christ'* (Ephesians 2:13).

Remission Of Sin

God gave a picture of what He would do with the blood of Jesus, in the Old Testament when He spoke these words to the Israelites.

> *For the life of the flesh is in the blood: and I have given it to you upon the altar to make an atonement for your souls: for it is the blood that maketh an atonement for the soul.*
>
> (Leviticus 17:11)

It is the blood that makes atonement for the soul. It is the blood alone that can redeem the soul of a man that has gone astray from God. Without the shedding of blood there is no remission of sin, there is no forgiveness (Hebrews 9:22).

In the Old Testament, before Jesus' atoning death, it was the blood of goats, sheep, bulls and other animals that was used to atone for sins. This was just a shadow of the blood of Jesus that was yet to be shed. To atone means to cover. With the blood of these animals they could appease God and cover their sins before His holy eyes – because He is *of purer eyes than to behold evil* (Habakkuk 1:13).

It is very significant that although the word 'atone' or 'atonement' occurs forty-eight times in the Old Testament, it never really occurs in the New Testament. In Romans 5:11 where the King James translation put 'atonement' the correct translation is 'reconciliation'. The reason is obvious. The blood of Jesus Christ remits, it does not just atone for or cover our sins, it blots out, cancels them and makes us new creatures in Christ. *'For this is my blood of the new testament, which is shed for many for the remission of sins'* (Matthew 26:28).

Under this old covenant, the people received forgiveness of sins, they had their sins covered; God did not impute to them any iniquity when they shed the blood of these animals as He commanded them. The limit of their experience is described by David.

> *Blessed is he whose transgression is forgiven,*
> *   whose sin is covered.*
> *Blessed is the man unto whom the LORD*
> *   imputeth not iniquity,*
> *And in whose spirit there is no guile.*
>
> (Psalm 32:1–2)

It was a matter of forbearance. God did not forgive them just because they offered the blood of animals as He commanded. It was not that the power of sin was broken and destroyed in their lives. It was not that they received the righteousness of God in their spirits. It was not that they could be made new creatures. The blood of bulls and goats could not make anyone perfect. But God permitted it because the Perfect Sacrifice was yet to come.

Now God has caused the blood of Jesus Christ to be shed, not only to cover our sins but also to blot them out and impart His righteousness into us.

To remit means to blot out, to purge, to cleanse. Whereas the blood of the Old Testament could only atone for or cover sin, the blood of the New Testament is to remit sins. The blood of Jesus is the blood of the New Testament. The blood of Jesus is able to break the power of sin over your life, purge your conscience from guilt, and save you from the guilt and consequences of sin, so that you are able to worship and serve the living God freely and acceptably. When we are washed in the blood of Jesus, our case with God is no longer a matter of forbearance but a matter of grace. We are loved and accepted in the beloved Son of God, we are not just tolerated.

For if the blood of bulls and of goats, and the ashes of an heifer sprinkling the unclean, sanctifieth to the purifying of the flesh: how much more shall the blood of Christ, who through the eternal Spirit offered himself without spot to God, purge your conscience from dead works to serve the living God?

(Hebrews 9:13–14)

This is not all that the blood of Jesus does, there is much more.

Saved From Wrath To Come

We were sinners, worthy of nothing but the righteous judgment and the fearful wrath of God. It is the blood of Jesus that saves us from the wrath to come. We need not be afraid of God's wrath that is coming upon the world as we are living under this blood. We are not called to wrath but to salvation (I Thessalonians 5:9).

> *Much more then, being now justified by his blood, we shall be saved from wrath through him. For if, when we were enemies, we were reconciled to God by the death of his Son, much more, being reconciled, we shall be saved by his life.*
>
> (Romans 5:9–10)

We were rebels, far from God and separated from the hope of eternal life. We were not in fellowship with Him. The thought of God and His righteous judgment was a terror to us. But now we have been brought near God through the blood of Jesus Christ – united with Him in vital relationship and fellowship. God is no longer just our God but also our Father, because we have trusted in the blood of Jesus.

When Jesus rose from the dead – being the High Priest of our profession, He was to ascend to God and present His blood in the Holy of Holies to perfect the offering for our sins – He said these words to Mary:

> *Touch me not; for I am not yet ascended to my Father: but go to my brethren, and say unto them,*

I ascend unto my Father, and your Father; and to my God, and your God.

(John 20:17)

God is my Father. I have been brought near to God, through the blood of Jesus Christ – Alleluia!

Redeemed By The Blood

We have been redeemed from the power of darkness by the blood of Jesus Christ. We were slaves under the devil. He did whatever he pleased with us. He could make us get drunk, curse, fornicate and lie. He could lay all manner of sicknesses on us. He caused us to go into debt and live in anxiety and fear – we were his property. Adam sold us to him.

But a price was paid for us; Jesus shed His blood to pay the price for our redemption. With this blood He redeemed us to God that we might no longer be under servitude to the devil. The moment we accept Him as our Lord and Saviour and trust in His blood for our cleansing, we are transferred from the kingdom of darkness – the kingdom of the devil, into the Kingdom of God. When you are in the Kingdom of God, the devil has no right over you. He no longer has any dominion over you. You belong to God, the devil cannot do whatever he likes with you – spirit, soul and body. Jesus has set you free by His blood. Stand in this, your liberty, and be no longer entangled in the yoke of bondage.

Giving thanks unto the Father, which hath made us meet to be partakers of the inheritance of the

saints in light: who hath delivered us from the
power of darkness, and hath translated us into
the kingdom of his dear Son: in whom we have
redemption through his blood, even the forgive-
ness of sins.

(Colossians 1:12–14)

Justified By The Blood

We are justified by the blood of Jesus. Righteousness
is both imputed and imparted to our spirit. It is the
imputed righteousness that gives us a right standing
before God; it is the imparted righteousness that makes
us live a holy and radiant life, bringing forth the fruit of
righteousness by the grace of God. All this by the blood
of Jesus, the Lamb of God (Romans 5:9).

If truly you have trusted in the blood of Jesus Christ
and you are born again, you have *imputed* righteousness. You have right-standing with God. As far as God
is concerned you are righteous. He no longer sees you
in your former state of sin and unworthiness. He now
sees you in Christ, washed and covered by His blood.
You are accepted in the Beloved (Ephesians 1:6).

Also, you have *imparted* righteousness. By the blood
of Jesus Christ, the very life and nature of God has
been imparted to you in the inner man, in your spirit.
You have been made a partaker of the divine nature
(II Peter 1:4). This nature of God that is imparted to
you is all righteousness, all holiness, purity, love and
power. It cannot sin at all – Ephesians 4:24; Colossians
3:10; I John 3:9. This is what activates and enables us
to walk in holiness and righteousness all the days of
our lives. God does not just forgive our sins and

leave us to struggle on to be holy. Holiness does not come by struggling. But He imparts His very nature and righteousness into us by the Holy Spirit. So long as we listen to and yield to the prompting of this life and Spirit of God within us, we are able to overcome all temptations; not walking in the flesh but walking in the Spirit.

And that ye put on the new man, which after God is created in righteousness and true holiness.

(Ephesians 4:24)

Free Access To God By The Blood

It is by the blood that we have access to God directly, in the name of Jesus. This is a glorious privilege that we have as children of the living God. We can enter into the Holy of Holies directly, anytime, and have sweet communion with God. There is no barrier, no veil between us. The Father is there happily waiting to receive us, His children. Jesus Christ is there at the right hand of the Majesty, faithfully representing us, pleading our case and ensuring that all that we desire according to His will is made good.

In the Old Testament, nobody could enter into the Holy of Holies, except the High Priest. And he could only enter covered by the blood of animals, once a year. (Suppose you had just one chance in the year to pray to God!) But when Jesus died, the veil of the inner temple broke into two, the way was made plain and open into the presence of God. Now you can enter in and have fellowship, anytime, any day. And we are accepted in the Beloved. This is why we are asked to come into the holy presence of God with boldness. Not as beggars, not

as paupers, not as orphans, but with boldness, by the
blood of Jesus.

> *Having therefore, brethren, boldness to enter into
> the holiest by the blood of Jesus, by a new and
> living way, which he hath consecrated for us,
> through the veil, that is to say, his flesh; and
> having an high priest over the house of God; let
> us draw near with a true heart in full assurance
> of faith, having our hearts sprinkled from an evil
> conscience, and our bodies washed with pure
> water.*
>
> (Hebrews 10:19–22)

We have a High Priest. We have the blood of covering.
We have a loving Father. Let us go in to Him with
boldness and make our petition known.

When a child of God knows all these benefits that
belong to him through the blood of Jesus that was shed
for him, and he walks in the consciousness of the reality
of these things, he will not only be a victor, but a terror
to the devil. This is why the devil will try to keep a child
of God from knowing these facts. When he sees that
he cannot keep you from knowing them, then real war
starts. Therefore, it is good for us to know the devices
of the devil and not fall into his traps.

Do Not Listen To The Accuser

The first thing he will do to keep a child of God from
moving forward and making progress, is to haunt him
with the memory of past sins and failures, with feelings
of guilt and condemnation over sins already confessed
with all honesty, and with the blood of Jesus pleaded

with all earnestness. The devil will make the sins as
real as if the blood of Jesus did not avail in cleansing
them. It can make you feel constantly guilty, thus
rendering you ineffective in God's service. In some
cases, this experience can degenerate into depression
and despair.

If you live in the consciousness of your past, which
you have sincerely committed to God, the devil will
always whip you. You do not need to listen to the devil.
He is *the accuser of the brethren*. Thanks be to God,
we can overcome him.

How? It is by the blood of the Lamb and by the Word
of God. You know that the blood of Jesus cleanses sin.
The blood of Jesus is the blood of the new covenant.

This is the covenant that I will make with them
After those days, saith the Lord,
I will put my laws into their hearts,
And in their minds will I write them;
And their sins and iniquities will I remember no
*   more.*

(Hebrews 10:16–17)

God does not remember your past sins anymore once
you have genuinely repented. He has forgiven and He
has forgotten. This fact is stated again and again in
the Scriptures. (Isaiah 43:25; Jeremiah 31:34; Romans
11:27; Hebrews 8:12).

I, even I, am he that blotteth out thy transgres-
sions for mine own sake, and will not remem-
ber thy sins. Put me in remembrance: let us
plead together: declare thou, that thou mayest
be justified.

(Isaiah 43:25–26)

This is because of the blood of Jesus. Through this blood, your burden of sins have been forgiven and forgotten and you have been cleansed. Your sins are in the sea of God's forgetfulness. Do not go about searching for them again. Whenever the enemy comes with these terrible experiences of the past, hold the blood of Jesus against him and use the Word of God. You will have victory over the enemy and enjoy unruffled peace.

Victory In Temptation

The blood of the Lord Jesus also gives us victory over temptation and sin. This is one big area of the work of the devil. We are surrounded with demons seeking to break our fellowship with the Father, to cause us to fall into sin and walk in darkness. Various things are used to tempt us – lust, pride, covetousness, evil thoughts, hatred, immoralities, greed, love of money, and many others. How do we live a holy and blameless life, overcoming these various temptations of the devil? By living in constant fellowship with the Father, under the blood of Jesus Christ.

> *But if we walk in the light, as he is in the light, we have fellowship one with another, and the blood of Jesus Christ his Son cleanseth us from all sin.*
>
> (I John 1:7)

The blood avails as we fellowship with the Father – constant and unbroken fellowship – and the blood cleanses us from all that would separate us from the Father.

This is the provision of God for our continuous sanctification and holiness. He causes the blood to keep us clean, to keep us from contamination. Continuously, we are being cleansed from our sins. This is why it is impossible for the devil to cause us to sin without our consent. It is only when we consent to the devil and submit our will to temptation, that we sin. Otherwise, the blood keeps purifying us, thereby making us holy and blameless before God. This can be a constant experience of a child of God. *'My little children, these things write I unto you, that ye sin not'* (I John 2:1). When you are faced with a temptation, know that the adversary is around wanting you to fall and displease God our Father. Determine that you are not going to fall. Ask for God's help. Plead the blood of Jesus Christ. Resist and rebuke the particular demon behind that temptation and claim your victory by the blood. *'Resist the devil, and he will flee from you'* (James 4:7).

But what happens if a believer sins?

This should be actually the exception. It is like having an accident with your car, if you do have one it is not every day. It is only the careless driver that will frequently have accidents. Likewise it is the careless Christian that will frequently fall into sin.

Yet God has made provision, also through the blood of Jesus, to cleanse any believer who falls into sin, if he will confess his sins and ask to be cleansed in the blood of Jesus.

My little children, these things write I unto you, that ye sin not. And if any man sin, we have an advocate with the Father, Jesus Christ the righteous: and he is the propitiation for our sins:

and not for ours only, but also for the sins of the whole world.

(I John 2:1–2)

Jesus is the propitiation – that is, the sacrifice that takes away our sins. He did it by His blood. Hence, when we miss God and fall into sin let us plead the blood, confessing our sins and we shall be cleansed again and brought into fellowship with God. *'If we confess our sins, he is faithful and just to forgive us our sins, and to cleanse us from all unrighteousness'* (I John 1:9). You will see that God binds the forgiveness and cleansing of the sins we confess to His faithfulness and justice. That is the grace of God. It is only when He ceases to be faithful and just that He will cease to forgive sins that are covered in the blood of Christ.

You will see that God has made adequate provision for us to overcome the devil, in whatever way he wants to use sin to weaken us and ruin our fellowship with God. Be it past sins or present temptations or failures, the blood is efficacious and we can always walk in victory.

Many Christians are living with terrible guilty consciences. Past sins weigh them down. Present temptations beset them. Use the weapon God has given you and continue to walk under the blood of Jesus Christ, in holiness and righteousness all the days of your life. And the devil can do you no harm.

There hath no temptation taken you but such as is common to man: but God is faithful, who will not suffer you to be tempted above that ye are able; but will with the temptation also make a way to escape, that ye may be able to bear it.

(I Corinthians 10:13)

Protection By The Blood

As we look at its protective power, we see the blood covers us and protects us from all evil. This is what happened to the children of Israel in Egypt when the angel of destruction destroyed all the first-born of the Egyptians. The Israelites were covered under the blood, and because of this the angel of destruction could not come near them.

We should realise the protective power of the blood of Jesus Christ and take advantage of it. The blood protects us from plagues, epidemics and destructive diseases. The blood protects us from demonic invasion, oppression and afflictions. We should not allow Satan to lay anything evil on us. We should constantly plead the blood of Jesus Christ and obtain our victory.

There is a hedge that God has made around His people. This is the type of a hedge He made around Job, such that the devil could not touch him without permission (Job 1:10). This hedge is made of the blood of Jesus Christ. Hence the devil cannot touch you if you remain perpetually under that blood. *'And when I see the blood, I will pass over you, and the plague shall not be upon you to destroy you'* (Exodus 12:13).

But it is good to sound a warning here. When we go outside the coverage of the blood of Jesus ... into sin and disobedience and backsliding, we allow in the serpent to bite us. *'He that diggeth a pit shall fall into it; and whoso breaketh an hedge, a serpent shall bite him'* (Ecclesiastes 10:8).

This was the case of a sister I met recently. She knew the Lord and was a fervent believer, but she allowed herself to fall in love with an unbeliever. And despite the warning of the Scriptures, not to be unequally yoked with an unbeliever, she decided that this man

was so wonderful she must disobey the Lord and marry
him. Soon after the marriage everything came tumbling
down. She lost the joy of salvation, the marriage was
in trouble, and she eventually turned totally from the
Lord. The devil really afflicted her because she was
not staying under the blood. Eventually she realised
that it was the Lord alone who could deliver her from
satanic affliction, so she returned to the Lord and was
graciously restored. Stay under the blood and do not
break the hedge.

The blood brings victory against demonic attacks.
These attacks can take various forms – accidents, fear,
sickness, sudden oppression in sleep. Whatever form
the satanic attacks take, plead the blood of Jesus and
the demons will flee.

Often the devil tries to hinder the blessings of God.
We overcome this by pleading the blood of Jesus. Many
times at the start of a meeting I perceive the presence
of evil spirits trying to hinder the movement of God.
I either start pleading the blood of Jesus or lead the
congregation in doing so, and a breakthrough occurs
immediately. I have asked believers who found it tough
receiving the baptism in the Holy Spirit to plead the
blood of Jesus and they received this gift from God
almost instantaneously. The same applies for other
blessings including financial. Furthermore, when you
find it difficult to obtain a definite breakthrough in
prayer, plead the blood, and victory shall come. No
matter what satanic attack it is you are experiencing
and in whatever aspect of your life, plead the blood and
your victory is certain.

Finally, the devil himself knows that it was the blood
of Jesus that finished him on Calvary. The blood broke
his dominion over man and rendered him powerless.
The saints who will overcome and reign with Jesus

should learn to use the blood in conjunction with the words of their testimony. Thus the devil will be defeated and the saints will live in high victory. This is a weapon God has provided for us, the efficacy of which cannot fail.

And they overcame him by the blood of the Lamb, and by the word of their testimony; and they loved not their lives unto the death.

(Revelation 12:11)

Chapter Eight

The Word Of God

The Word of God is the direct projection of His personality as well as the expression of His thought. Therefore the Word of God is as potent as God Himself. It is both a protective covering (armour) as well as an offensive weapon in spiritual warfare. It is called the sword of the Spirit. '*And take the helmet of salvation, and the sword of the Spirit, which is the word of God*' (Ephesians 6:17).

There is no possibility of overcoming the enemy and his hosts without the Word of God. Knowing that your victory in spiritual warfare as well as your usefulness in the hand of the Lord depends to a large extent on your attitude to the Word of God should definitely make you take another look at the Bible – the Word of God.

The Lord told Joshua, immediately after he assumed the leadership of the nation of Israel, that for him to be successful he had to pay good attention to the Word.

This book of the law shall not depart out of thy mouth; but thou shalt meditate therein day and night, that thou mayest observe to do according to all that is written therein: for then thou shalt make thy way prosperous, and then thou shalt have good success.

(Joshua 1:8)

God's formula for success in life and spiritual endeavour has not changed. It is still the Word of God. To develop strong faith and spiritual stamina you need to spend time meditating on it daily.

When we talk of the Word of God, it may refer to either of the following.

Logos And Rhema

There is the Word Incarnate – the Greek term for this is Logos – the Word that was made flesh. The apostle John writes about this in John 1:1–14 and I John 1:1–4. This is actually the revelation of Himself that God gave to man in the Person of our Lord Jesus Christ, the Living Word of God.

In the beginning was the Word, and the Word was with God, and the Word was God. The same was in the beginning with God. All things were made by him; and without him was not any thing made that was made. In him was life; and the life was the light of men. And the light shineth in darkness; and the darkness comprehended it not. . . .

And the Word was made flesh, and dwelt among us, (and we beheld his glory, the glory as of the only begotten of the Father,) full of grace and truth.

(John 1:1–5, 14)

That which was from the beginning, which we have heard, which we have seen with our eyes, which we have looked upon, and our hands have handled, of the Word of life; (for the life was manifested, and we have seen it, and bear witness, and

*shew unto you that eternal life, which was with the
Father, and was manifested unto us;) that which
we have seen and heard declare we unto you, that
ye also may have fellowship with us: and truly
our fellowship is with the Father, and with his
Son Jesus Christ.*

(I John 1:1–3)

There is the written Word of God. This is the revelation that God gave of Himself that was written
down in the Bible by the inspiration of the Holy
Spirit. It comprises the thirty-nine books of the Old
Testament and the twenty-seven books of the New
Testament taken together. They constitute the valid
and infallible revelation of God to man and are the
final authority in every matter of Christian faith and
conduct.

*No prophecy of the scripture is of any private
interpretation. For the prophecy came not in old
time by the will of man: but holy men of God spake
as they were moved by the Holy Ghost.*

(II Peter 1:20–21)

*All scripture is given by inspiration of God, and is
profitable for doctrine, for reproof, for correction,
for instruction in righteousness: that the man of
God may be perfect, throughly furnished unto all
good works.*

(II Timothy 3:16–17)

There is the spoken or quickened Word of God – Rhema.
This is the Word of God as inspired by the Holy Spirit
to meet a particular situation, and *'No word from God
shall be void of power'* (Luke 1:37 Amplified).

The incarnate Word came into the world, accomplished our redemption, rose from the dead after three days, ascended to the right hand of the Father from where He shall come again in the same way that He went.

The written Word – from Genesis to Revelation, is to be read by us, and through the help of the Holy Spirit, is quickened to meet our needs. As it is written it is lifeless without the quickening of the Holy Spirit. But when we apply the Word under the unction of the Holy Spirit it works effectually. The Word is a mighty weapon of spiritual warfare when the Spirit of God quickens and gives it life. That is why we must depend on the Holy Spirit both to open our understanding to the Word and to quicken the Word to and in us. *'It is the spirit that quickeneth; the flesh profiteth nothing: the words that I speak unto you, they are spirit, and they are life'* (John 6:63).

W. E. Vine, the Bible scholar, has this to say:

The significance of Rhema (as distinct from Logos) is exemplified in the injunction to take 'the sword of the Spirit, which is the word of God' (Ephesians 6:17). Here the reference is not to the whole Bible as such, but to the individual scripture which the Spirit brings to our remembrance for use in time of need, a prerequisite being the regular storing of the mind with scripture.[1]

Power In The Word

Has it ever happened to you, that while you are studying the Scriptures a verse suddenly 'jumps at you' and the Spirit of God begins to explain that verse to you, relating it to your situation very specifically? Or as you read the Bible a verse or a portion comes alive as if you have never come across it before? It may even be a whole chapter. The Holy Spirit opens your understanding to the message in the chapter and uses the Word to meet your specific needs. That is the quickened Word at work in you. You may even be listening to an anointed preacher or be reading an anointed message and it appears as if there is a force working in you, moving you to take a step of faith or act along certain lines. That again is Rhema, the creative Word of God at work in you. This happens from time to time as we depend on the Holy Spirit to quicken the Word of God to and in us.

It is the Word of God that gives life, power, inspiration and grace. It is the Word that saves and heals and delivers. It is the Word that cleanses and keeps the heart pure. The Word also edifies, anoints and strengthens. There is power in the Word of God.

This is the weapon the Lord has given us in fighting against the devil. It is quick, it is powerful. It is irresistible. It can slay every enemy of righteousness, for it is the 'sword of the Spirit' (Ephesians 6:17). It can break the hardest of hearts and consume anything that is opposed to God because it is like fire and like a hammer that breaks the rock to pieces (Jeremiah 23:29). It can search deep into the hearts of men, and bring out all the hidden things, because it is the revealer of men's hearts. Many people have shared testimonies of how they sat under anointed preachings and it was as if the preacher knew all their secrets. That is the Word of God at work. This mighty weapon that is irresistible in its working, God has committed into our hands, to use effectively in spiritual warfare.

For the word of God is quick, and powerful, and sharper than any twoedged sword, piercing even to the dividing asunder of soul and spirit, and of the joints and marrow, and is a discerner of the thoughts and intents of the heart. Neither is there any creature that is not manifest in his sight: but all things are naked and opened unto the eyes of him with whom we have to do.

(Hebrews 4:12–13)

Using The Word In Conflicts

It is the Word of God that gives us victory in the battles of life. We cannot defeat the devil by using human wisdom, theories and philosophies. But with the Word of God the devil is beaten flat on his face; he has no answer to it. That is why we should always be prepared, with a word from the Bible, to use in times of crisis.

Suppose the devil comes around to tempt you to commit adultery. You should readily use verses like *'the body is not for fornication, but for the Lord'* (I Corinthians 6:13; also Exodus 20:14; Proverbs 6:32; II Timothy 2:22). Suppose he comes around with evil and dirty thoughts, you should use a word like II Corinthians 10:3–5 and get rid of those thoughts. If he brings a sickness on your body or on that of a loved one – by His stripes you were healed (I Peter 2:24; Exodus 15:25–26; Psalm 103:1–3). The enemy may come in many different ways, but the Word of God should so dwell in us that we should be able to overcome him no matter how subtle his attack. It was the Word that Jesus Christ used to defeat the enemy in the wilderness. And this Word is also available to us today.

One morning I woke up early with a great fear in my heart. Strange, isn't it? Sometimes I wake up with a song, or a prayer, either in the spirit or with understanding. Other times, I wake up with a burden to pray; but this morning, I woke up with fear. I first lay quietly in my bed listening to what the Holy Spirit would say to my spirit. Nothing. The fear increased. My heart was pounding fast. I could not pray. I got out of bed and knelt down. I prayed in tongues for a while and then kept quiet to listen to the Spirit of God in me.

The Spirit then whispered: *'What time I am afraid, I will trust in thee . . . lead me to the rock that is higher than I'* (Psalm 56:3; 61:2). I knew the Holy Spirit had joined two verses from the Psalms to meet my need. I didn't know where exactly they were, but I began to confess these words again and again. Later, I got up to go to the bathroom with my pocket Bible. There I started to search the Psalms to find these verses. As I was doing this the Spirit led me to Psalm 46, which I read. It met my heart's need exactly. The fear just vanished immediately. My heart was light, and I began to worship and praise the Lord. Next, I went into solid praying. The devil really suffered that morning! I was filled with the joy of the Lord. Glory be to God. It was the Word that the Lord used to deal with the devil who wanted to weigh me down with fear and sorrow.

We can allow the Holy Spirit to quicken the Word in us to meet whatever our need might be in any particular situation. As long as a man rests on the Word of God, he is invincible, impregnable and immovable. *'They that trust in the LORD shall be as mount Zion, which cannot be removed, but abideth for ever'*

(Psalm 125:1). Satan cannot touch them; rather they are the most serious menace to all satanic devices, plans, plots and schemes. To them has been given power over all the power of the enemy. There is not any reinforcement which the prince of darkness can order from the lowest depths of his dark domain for which those who believe God's Word are not more than a match. '*No weapon that is formed against thee shall prosper*' (Isaiah 54:17). Whatever it is that the enemy tries, we are perfectly safe so long as we are abiding in the Word of God and the Word of God is abiding in us.

The Word In Preaching

The devil does not fear a minister that does not preach the Word. Those that declare nothing but the Word of God hit him really hard and put him to flight in the lives of people.

Kenneth E. Hagin said that at the beginning of his ministry he used to preach the Word of God mixed in with the philosophies of men and a lot of story telling. He said it did not work. Men were not being blessed. After sometime, according to him, he decided to preach nothing but the Word of God. It was a tough thing to do, but he kept at it. Then souls were saved, people were healed, there were deliverances, people were edified and filled with the Holy Spirit. You see it is the Word of God that blesses men.

We should preach nothing but the Word. Tell it as it is. Do not mind the reasoning of men or their philosophies. If we faithfully preach the Word, it will work.

The law of the LORD is perfect, converting the soul:
The testimony of the LORD is sure, making wise the
simple.

(Psalm 19:7)

Do not water down the Word. Do not bend it to suit
men. And do not shy away from preaching it. This is
not just to preachers and teachers of the Gospel but to
all Christians as witnesses for Christ.

I charge thee therefore before God, and the Lord
Jesus Christ, who shall judge the quick and the
dead at his appearing and his kingdom; preach
the word; be instant in season, out of season;
reprove, rebuke, exhort with all longsuffering
and doctrine.

(II Timothy 4:1–2)

Many of us even shy away from preaching the Word
to our friends. There is no other way people could be
saved but through the Word of God. It is the power of
God for the salvation of those that believe. When we
preach we pierce the devil. Preaching the Gospel of
peace is wearing our sandals and treading on serpents,
scorpions, and all the power of the enemy (Luke 10:19;
Ephesians 6:15). If we preach nothing but the Word of
God, under the anointing of the Holy Spirit, many souls
will be saved, healed, delivered and edified greatly. And
the Lord will confirm the Word with many signs and
miracles.

If in preaching we make our success the success of the
Word of God and declare it boldly and wholly we shall
experience tremendous success to the glory of God. This
is one key secret behind the success of Billy Graham,

the world-renowned evangelist. Just listen to him or read any of his messages and notice how frequently this phrase, 'The Bible says', occurs. That man stands for the Bible and proclaims it boldly, and it works. Let us preach nothing but the Word of God.

Using The Word In Prayer

Prayer becomes very effectual when we use the Word of God. When you listen to some folks pray, their prayers are very light and unforceful, spiritually. But studying the prayers of the saints of God that are recorded in the Bible, we find that they effectively used the promises of God. They quoted God's Word back to Him. And when we pray that way, holding on to the Word of God and reminding Him of His promises we are bound to prevail.

Take for instance, the case of Moses, when he was interceding for the children of Israel because of their sin. He reminded God of His covenant (His Word to their fathers). *'Remember Abraham'*, said Moses, *'Isaac and Israel, thy servants, to whom thou swarest by thine own self, and saidst unto them ...'* and he prevailed. Likewise, the early disciples, when they were praying, held onto God and His Word. 'Lord,' they prayed, *'thou art God, which hast made heaven, and earth, and sea, and all that in them is: Who by the mouth of thy servant David hast said, ...'* Thus they continued to pray, standing on the promises of God. They received speedy answers and got their hearts' desires.

Let us learn to use the Word in prayer. It makes our prayers forceful and effectual. Do you have a prayer burden or desire? Look into the Bible and find relevant promises you can use to press your case and prevail over the enemy. Meditate a little on those promises and then go to God and ask according to His Word. Praying like this will never fail to get results.

If ye abide in me, and my words abide in you, ye shall ask what ye will, and it shall be done unto you.

(John 15:7)

Let His Word abide in you. Then you will ask whatever you desire and it shall be granted.

The Word In Ministering Deliverance

It is the Word of God, spoken under the anointing of the Holy Spirit that brings deliverance to people. It may be deliverance from sin, or sickness, or demonic bondage or fear.

Whatever is the work of the enemy, the Word of God is a sufficient weapon to deal with it. '*He sent his word, and healed them, And delivered them from their destructions*' (Psalm 107:20).

Once we were ministering to a man who was demon-possessed. The demons reacted violently and showed that they were not going to go out. I then proceeded to attack them with the Word of God:

Firstly, this body is the temple of the Holy Ghost and not of demons (I Corinthians 6:19).

Secondly, demons have no right to possess man — they are strangers in human bodies. And the Bible says, '*The strangers shall fade away, and be afraid out of their close places*' (Psalm 18:45).

Thirdly, Jesus Christ has given me authority to cast out demons, and they must obey. *'In my name shall they cast out devils'* (Mark 16:17).

As I spoke those words, the anointing of the Holy Spirit came upon me. The Word took effect and the strongest of the demons left. The others soon followed, as we continuously used the Word to drive them out.

Let us learn to effectively use the weapons that God has provided for us. Let us study, meditate on and read the Word of God. We must soak ourselves in the Word of God so much that it will be at work in and through us. Let us live by the Word of God. Let us speak the Word constantly thereby punching the devil hard and dealing with all the enemies of righteousness.

Exceeding Growing Faith

The best way for your faith to grow and for you to live a successful Christian life is by meditating on the Word of God and acting on it. Do not just read it – study it. Do not stop at studying – meditate on it until it becomes a part of you. Do not stop there either; go forward and act on the Word of God. Dr E. W. Kenyon puts this helpfully:

> There is but one foundation for faith, the Living Word. As we become one with the Word in our actions, then faith becomes an unconscious reality. You never think of faith, you only think of the need and His ability to meet it. If you wish faith to grow and become robust and strong, soak in the Word, feed on it, meditate on it, until you become one with it in the sense that you are one with your business.[2]

Find out what you are in Christ, what your privileges are, what He thinks of you, what He says of you. You will find all these in the Word.

Get into the Word, and use it to win in the battle of life. This is the way to make your faith grow exceedingly. And since faith is the victory that overcomes, you are sure to be more than a conqueror.

> *Let the word of Christ dwell in you richly in all wisdom; teaching and admonishing one another in psalms and hymns and spiritual songs, singing with grace in your hearts to the Lord.*
>   (Colossians 3:16)

Chapter Nine

The Weapon Of Prayer

Volumes have been written on prayer that have blessed the Church of the Lord Jesus. But very few people have seen prayer as a weapon of war that we use to whip the devil and his cohorts.

Many see prayer only as a means of getting our needs met, and perhaps that of others. Prayer means more than that. It is an irresistible weapon. The destinies of nations, cities, communities, congregations and individuals have been changed, and wicked plans of the enemy squashed, by the prayer of faith offered by the people of God.

Abraham drew near and pleaded boldly with God over Sodom and Gomorrha. Moses averted the wrath of God which was coming upon the sinning people of Israel when they were in the wilderness, because he prayed. Samuel was such a notable intercessor that God had high regard for him: and his words never fell to the ground. These examples should be a challenge to us.

Even Jesus our Lord struggled with the devil in the Garden of Gethsemane and won by using the unfailing weapon of prayer.

The apostles valued this weapon so much that they said: *'But we will give ourselves continually to prayer and to the ministry of the word'* (Acts 6:4). In the early

Church, many of the apostles (James, for example) had calloused knees from waiting on the Lord in prayers of faith. O that saints would stir themselves up again to lay hold of God, demanding wonders and signs in the name of Jesus! That you would shake yourself awake, strengthen your feeble knees and seek the face of God, in believing prayers. The prophet Isaiah lamented: '*And there is none that calleth upon thy name, that stirreth up himself to take hold of thee* ... ' (Isaiah 64:7). The weapon of prayer is available for your free use. Stir yourself up and lay hold of the Lord.

There is no man that can be much for God excepting that man that is much with God. It is by waiting on the Lord and praying that we always get our strength renewed. It is then we can do exploits for God. This is the secret of the men that have been used of God in the past to shake nations, revive the Church and win multitudes for Christ Jesus the Lord. Martin Luther was such a man. He remarked that no matter how busy a day, he would spend the first three hours of the day with God in prayer. He broke the chains of papacy, brought into light the truth of justification by faith and prevailed against the devil and all his hosts trying to stop him from doing the will of God. Wesley was another such man, who although he had a difficult wife, said that she only succeeded in causing him always to be on his knees in prayer. Despite his unstable family he was not deterred from praying, rather it drove him to be closer to God. He used the weapon of prayer, fought the good fight of faith and finished his job.

Charles G. Finney has been described as the most successful evangelist that has lived since the apostles. Records have it that over 500,000 souls were converted through the direct labour of this anointed man of God, with over 80 per cent abiding, that is, becoming mature, responsible believers; and that many hundreds of young men and women went into the work of the ministry under his labour of love. This he did, when there was no mass media, public address system, radio or television to spread the Gospel. How did he do it? By prayers of faith. He always asked Christians to join him in prayer and it was said that 'he almost prayed himself to death'.

There are other well-known praying men of God like John Knox, Alexander Dowie, David Brainerd and John (praying) Hyde. In their days they used the weapon of prayer to accomplish great things and to bring glory to God. Mary, Queen of Scots, was quoted as saying 'I fear the prayers of John Knox more than all the armies of England'. Such were the exploits of these great men of God through prayer. They are all gone to be with the Lord. But we are alive here on earth. This is our day. Let us stir ourselves up to pray. If we do as they did we shall get the results that they got, and even better results because these are the days of the latter rain.

The Prayer Of Faith

You can clear the devil out of your path and put him perpetually under your feet, by making use of your prayer of faith. The devil will always want to obstruct your ways. He does not want you to have victory. He wants you to stumble and fall – either into sin, or error or another snare. You can only overcome him by watching and praying. *'Watch and pray, that ye enter not into temptation'* (Matthew 26:41). Every mountain that stands in your way to victory can be moved by your prayer of faith. Every problem can be properly dealt

with as you bow your head in prayer. Then your path
will be straight and there will not be any stumbling
block in you.

> *Wherefore lift up the hands which hang down, and
> the feeble knees; and make straight paths for your
> feet, lest that which is lame be turned out of the
> way; but let it rather be healed.*
>
> (Hebrews 12:12–13)

Getting Your Needs Met Through The Prayer Of Faith

You can always get your needs met by praying in faith.
The Lord does not want us to suffer want in as much
as we are His children. The human tradition, that we
should be poor and wretched, barely getting along, is
contrary to the Scriptures. The Word says: *'The young
lions do lack, and suffer hunger: but they that seek the
LORD shall not want any good thing.'* I would rather
believe the Word of God than the tradition of men.
Also, the Bible says this of the children of God, walking
consistently by faith according to the Gospel:

> *He shall dwell on high: his place of defence shall
> be the munitions of rocks: bread shall be given
> him; his waters shall be sure.*
>
> (Isaiah 33:16)

We can literally believe that and prove God true to His
Word. The devil is your adversary. He will want you
to live beggarly and in dire need – financially, socially,
materially or spiritually. If you allow him he will hold
your money and prevent other gifts God has given you

from getting to you. I have learnt to command the devil to take his hand off my blessings. Anytime I give that command, it works.

Today, many saints are in need of healing. You can receive this too, by prayers of faith and by commanding the devil, in Jesus' name, to take his hands off your health. The Lord wants you to be strong. His joy is to see you strong and healthy. You cannot glorify Him in sickness as much as you would in perfect health. Do not listen to any lies of the devil that it is the will of God that you remain sick. His thoughts toward us are always good.

> *For I know the thoughts that I think toward you, saith the LORD, thoughts of peace, and not of evil, to give you an expected end. Then shall ye call upon me, and ye shall go and pray unto me, and I will hearken unto you . . .*
>
> (Jeremiah 29:11–12)

Whatever your need, by using your weapon of prayer, you can have it met.

> *My God shall supply all your need according to his riches in glory by Christ Jesus.*
>
> (Philippians 4:19)

Praying For The Needs Of Others

You can cause the needs of others to be met by using your weapon of prayer.

There is nothing as delightful as praying for others in love and in faith, looking upon their needs as your own. There is no ministry that ranks with the ministry of intercession. Every Christian should take the work of intercession seriously, praying for the saints (according to Ephesians 6:18), praying for the younger ones in the Lord, praying for someone who shared his or her needs with you, praying for friends and loved ones far and near. It is something wonderful to see God bless other people because we prayed for them.

This is where many of us still need to learn some lessons. We do not have to be selfish. Neither do we have to be narrow-minded in our use of the weapon of prayer. Let us have an enlarged heart. Let us pray for people, definitely and believingly. There are many that are tottering under the weight of their burdens – family problems, personal problems, spiritual crisis, social disappointments, etc. There are many bleeding hearts, even among the people of God. And many times when we know of the burden people bear, instead of helping them in prayer we start gossiping about them. Let us stop it. Let us learn to walk in love. Let us learn to pray for others, bearing their burdens. *'Bear ye one another's burdens, and so fulfil the law of Christ'* (Galatians 6:2).

When you find out others' problems, sincerely pray for them as if the problems were yours. As you continue in this manner, the Holy Spirit Himself will cause you to come across cases of genuine need and problems to which you can provide a solution through your prayer of faith. He can do this by revelation, by impression, by the manifestation of any of the gifts of the Holy Spirit or His providential leadings.

Praying always with all prayer and supplication in the Spirit, and watching thereunto with all perseverance and supplication for all saints.
(Ephesians 6:18)

Extending The Kingdom Of God Through Prayers

You can extend the Kingdom of God by using your weapon of prayer. We have to make a conquest of the world. There are many sinners still in the grip of the devil – in bondage with sin and sickness. The world was made by God, for man to rule and dominate. Man surrendered the authority God gave him to the devil in the garden of Eden and came under Satan's dominion. Right from that time, the whole world has been under the wicked grip of the devil. The Lord Jesus came and paid the price of the redemption of humanity; He gave us the charge to conquer the whole world by the proclamation of the Gospel. The Gospel is to be preached throughout the whole world – men and women must be liberated. *'And Jesus came and spake unto them, saying, All power is given unto me in heaven and in earth. Go ye therefore, and teach all nations . . .'* (Matthew 28:18–19).

But how do we advance in this conquest? By the use of our weapons of prayer. We can cause the Word of God to run swiftly, obstacles to be removed, souls to be saved in multitudes, the preaching of the Gospel to be followed by signs and wonders, as we pray in faith. The need in the Church of Christ today, is of men and women who would take up this 'closet ministry', where they are not seen in the open, and by their prayer of faith cause the work of God to move by leaps and bounds.

You can be that man. You can be that woman. The Lord can commit to you the ministry of intercession. That may be your own realm of operation. You should not miss the perfect will of God for your life.

You can pray for sinners, individually, in pairs, as a family unit, as a community, or as a nation. Ask the

Father to open their understanding to the message of
the Gospel and save them. Command the devil to let go
of them. Ask that they be reached by the living Word of
God. Remove every obstacle and hindrance to their
being born again. Pray in faith and you will see the
result.

You can pray for men of God anointed to preach
the Gospel. Pray for them individually, and by name
whenever possible. Ask that the glorious vision of world
conquest for Christ that they have, be renewed and
brightened every day. Pray that they be strengthened
with might in the inner man by the Holy Spirit. Pray
for boldness, words, open doors, effective and fruitful
ministration of the Word. Resist every attempt of the
devil to bring about discouragement and command that
all his snares be removed from their way. Also, ask for
an abundant supply of all they need to make God's work
a success, and for grace to finish their work with joy. As
you pray that way you will see those men of God grow
stronger and stronger, doing exploits for the Lord, and
you will be a partaker of the joy of their success.

You can also pray for churches (that is, denominations), ministries, seminaries and all para-church
institutions. It is our daily duty to pray for our nations
asking that the will of God be done as it is being done
in heaven, that we may live a quiet and peaceable life
in all godliness and honesty. There are many ways of
using our weapon of prayer to extend the Kingdom of
God upon the earth.

> *Ask of me, and I shall give thee the heathen for*
> *thine inheritance,*
> *And the uttermost parts of the earth for thy*
> *possession.*
>
> (Psalm 2:8)

Enforcing The Victory Of Calvary Through Prayer

We are to enforce the victory of Calvary by using the weapon of prayer. That was divine strategy – the devil knew nothing about the plan of God. He incited the mob to kill Jesus, but by killing Jesus, the Lord of glory, the devil and his cohorts, who were the princes of this world, destroyed themselves. This is a mystery and a divine wisdom.

> *Howbeit we speak wisdom among them that are perfect: yet not the wisdom of this world, nor of the princes of this world, that come to nought: but we speak the wisdom of God in a mystery, even the hidden wisdom, which God ordained before the world unto our glory: which none of the princes of this world knew: for had they known it, they would not have crucified the Lord of glory.*

> (I Corinthians 2:6–8)

The devil and his princes have come to nought (dethroned, spoilt and stripped of power) because by His death and resurrection, Jesus defeated principalities and powers and made an open show of them, triumphing over them in it. See Colossians 2:14–15. Hence, the devil is defeated, spoiled, and judged. *'The prince of this world is judged'* (John 16:11). The divine sentence has been passed upon him. He, therefore, has no right to lord it over any creature of God.

Yet, there is a type of guerrilla warfare going on. The devil still behaves as one with authority. But as children of God knowing of his defeat, we enforce the victory of Calvary and command him to flee. *'Resist*

the devil, and he will flee from you' (James 4:7).
Any situation we see where the devil is seeking to
cause trouble or confusion – either demon possession,
oppression or obsession, a demonic attack, or any work
of the devil, we bring to bear upon the devil the weight
of the victory of Calvary. He has no option but to flee.
He knows that he was finished at Calvary. Let us use
this weapon well, liberating people from the bondage
of the devil. It is the will of God.

Confidence In Prayer

We have been talking about how we can use the weapon
of prayer, but how do we approach God when we pray?
Timidly? Beggarly? As orphans? With guilt and sin
consciousness? No! Nothing of the sort.

We are children of God. He loves us. He wants to have
fellowship with us. He wants us to feel free in His loving
presence. Prayer should not be a burden, it should be a
delight.

We are the righteousness of God in Christ Jesus,
God no longer sees us as ourselves, He sees us in
Christ Jesus. And we are complete in Jesus, standing
blameless before the Father to fellowship with Him.
One of the great hindrances to a robust prayer life is
sin-consciousness. This should not be so. There should
be son-consciousness instead. Indeed we were sinners.
But we are now forgiven, saved by grace, children of the
Most High God. And let us keep away from anything
that the devil can use to break our fellowship with
the Father. Therefore let us go before the Father in
confident assurance that He will hear us and answer
our prayers.

Let us therefore come boldly unto the throne of grace, that we may obtain mercy, and find grace to help in time of need.

(Hebrews 4:16)

Prayer Of Agreement

One very effective way of using the weapon of prayer to whip the devil, is by agreeing with other believers as we pray. We may be two, three or more. The essential thing is that there should be agreement in our spirits concerning the particular thing or things which we desire. And we should be very specific. When we pray like this, according to the will of God, all the demons in the whole universe joined together cannot stop that prayer from getting answered with great speed.

Verily I say unto you, Whatsoever ye shall bind on earth shall be bound in heaven: and whatsoever ye shall loose on earth shall be loosed in heaven. Again I say unto you, That if two of you shall agree on earth as touching any thing that they shall ask, it shall be done for them of my Father which is in Heaven.

(Matthew 18:18–19)

A brother met with me sometime ago and told me of some problems he was having. After some discussion over the Word of God, we agreed together that (1) the Lord should provide him with a job before the middle of April (it was already almost the end of March) (2) we agreed on the minimum amount he should be paid,

among other things. Early in May that same year, I saw
the brother again and he shared with me that God had
done all that we had agreed on. That (1) he got a job
miraculously by the beginning of April (within a week
of our prayer of agreement), no interview, nothing, they
just asked him to start. (2) He was being paid about
fifty naira (N50.00) a month *above* the minimum we
had agreed upon. Truly, *'[God] is able to do exceeding
abundantly above all that we ask or think'* (Ephesians
3:20).

Another brother, who is a close friend, called in on
me and shared how fresh and real Matthew 18:19 has
become to him since he got engaged to his spouse. He
told me that there was not a single prayer point that
the two of them had agreed upon that has not come to
pass. God is true to His Word.

There was a family that was broken up by the devil.
The wife joined an occult movement which brought real
commotion that ended up in the separation of the couple. They had two children; they were not enjoying their
rightful parental affection; the husband was missing
the partnership and love of his wife; the woman was
missing the protection and love of her husband. All of
them were suffering. Miraculously, in the midst of this,
the man was converted. One day he came to meet me.
After a lengthy discussion, we agreed on certain prayer
points, and we prayed in agreement. Shortly after, the
woman, who by then was threatening a divorce in order
to remarry, was converted and the family was happily
reunited.

We can begin to multiply testimonies. But what we
need is for saints to come together and pray in agreement on specific issues, personal, local or national. The
answer must and will come with speed. The Word of
God guarantees that.

Prayer And Positive Confession

Positive confession plays a vital role in receiving answers to our prayers of faith. We do not kneel down to pray with belief, and rise up talking doubts and negatives. Those doubts you express after prayer cancel the effect of your prayer.

Pray in faith. After praying, refuse to doubt but instead, keep believing and keep confessing that your prayer is answered. Confession brings possession. Be it healing, or financial or material needs. It may be prayer for others. Do not contradict the prayers you have offered by your careless words. Let your confession agree with your prayer. '*By thy words,*' Jesus said, '*thou shalt be justified, and by thy words thou shalt be condemned*' (Matthew 12:37).

This was the problem Charles G. Finney had with the Christians around him before his conversion. They were always praying for revival and, at the same time, complaining that revival did not come. He was confused. He had read the promises of Jesus to answer prayer. He then concluded that either the people were not Christians, or that they were not praying in faith, or that the Word of God was not true.

Do not be a confusionist. Agree with the Word of God in your confession. Confess into reality what you have asked in prayer.

Therefore, I say unto you, What things soever ye desire, when ye pray, believe that ye receive them, and ye shall have them.

(Mark 11:24)

Let us hold fast the profession of our faith without wavering; (for he is faithful that promised;).

(Hebrews 10:23)

Begin Now To Use This Weapon

I suppose we have talked a lot on this subject. It is time now to arise and begin to use this weapon with more audacity than you have had before.

Be totally sincere and open to God as you pray. Lay your heart bare before Him. Be confident in Him, for He is interested even in the minutest details of your life.

Secondly, be very simple in believing. Faith is not struggling. Just relax and lean on the Holy Spirit and begin to talk to God as a son talks with a loving father.

Thirdly, be very definite in your requests. If you pray definitely, you will receive answers.

Fourthly, stand on the Word of God. Find a promise in the written Word that you can lay hold of, and claim it. Hold this promise before God and ask for a confirmation of it as far as your need is concerned. God is faithful. He cannot deny His Word.

Do not allow doubt to stay in your heart at all. It is better to doubt your doubts and trust in the living God. Give God glory and praise. You have prayed. You have believed the Word. Begin to praise and worship until the answer is manifested. Then give God the praise.

Lastly, keep moving forward. Just because you prayed yesterday, or in the night, or this morning, does not mean you should not pray now. Pray without ceasing. That you have obtained a staggering answer just recently does not mean you should miss other opportunities. Do not allow past success to be a stumbling block in the way of your progress. Thank God for the past and move steadily forward. Let us use this God-given weapon to defeat the devil in every aspect, and bring glory to our God.

Chapter Ten

Biblical Fasting

God ordained fasting, that by it His children might prevail against the enemy.

During His earthly walk, the Lord Jesus Christ assured us that fasting is something Christians are to practise as a spiritual worship to God, as a personal preparation for spiritual services, and as a means of dealing with the devil. When He was preaching the sermon on the mount, He said, among other things;

Moreover when ye fast, be not, as the hypocrites, of a sad countenance: for they disfigure their faces, that they may appear unto men to fast. Verily I say unto you, They have their reward. But thou, when thou fastest, anoint thine head, and wash thy face; that thou appear not unto men to fast, but unto thy Father which is in secret: and thy Father, which seeth in secret, shall reward thee openly.

(Matthew 6:16–18)

When Jesus was asked on one occasion why His disciples did not fast, He replied:

Can the children of the bridechamber mourn, as long as the bridegroom is with them? but the days

will come, when the bridegroom shall be taken
from them, and then shall they fast.

(Matthew 9:15)

From these passages it is clear that we are to fast, when
necessary, especially now that He, the Bridegroom, is
no longer here with us physically. He said, *'When ye*
fast . . .' not *'if ye fast . . .'*. Also, we are not supposed
to publicise our fast before men. As much as possible,
it should be between us and the Lord. It is clear from
the passages that our fast is to be directed to the Lord
'and thy Father, which seeth in secret, shall reward
thee openly'. Therefore fasting is a spiritual worship
to God.

The early apostles often fasted. This is one of the
reasons why they made much spiritual progress. We
read of them that, *'They ministered to the Lord, and*
fasted', *'they . . . fasted and prayed'*, they were *'in*
fastings often' (Acts 13:2,3; II Corinthians 11:27). If
we want to be as effective as they were, and to get
the same results, we have to practise fasting. Many
Christians are yet to learn to use this weapon because
they cannot miss a single meal to take time to seek
the face of the Lord. And they wonder why they are
not strong in the Lord and effective in His service. It
is important for us to begin to fast and we shall see
that as a weapon it works effectually.

We Have To Fast

If we are to defeat the devil and destroy his works
speedily and steadily; if we are to do the works of Jesus
effectively and fruitfully, we have to fast. Once when
the disciples of Jesus were battling unsuccessfully with
a deaf and dumb demon, the Lord came and cast out the

demon with such ease and confidence that the disciples were astonished.

'*Why could not we cast him out?*' was their question. Jesus answered, '*Because of your unbelief*' (Matthew 17:20). He also told them how faith could be inspired and strengthened by prayer and fasting. '*Howbeit this kind goeth not out but by prayer and fasting*' (Matthew 17:21).

There are increased demonic activities in the world today. Demons attack individuals, homes, communities, churches and fellowship groups at an alarming rate, causing terrible and sometimes incurable diseases, family upheavals and broken homes, insanity and malady, disunity and rebellion, anarchy, lawlessness and strife. The only people who can deal with these demons and bring them under control are the born-again, Spirit-filled Christians, who are walking in fellowship with God.

The way we can bring them under control is by exercising the spiritual authority God has given us through the weapon of fasting and prayer.

You must not continue to put up with the works of the devil – in your body, in your spiritual life, in your home or in the fellowship. Aggressively attack the enemy. Take time to fast and pray and strengthen your faith and overcome the situation. '*Resist the devil, and he will flee from you*' (James 4:7). This is not to say that without fasting you cannot overcome the situation, but fasting is a very important weapon in your hands. Use it effectively.

Reasons For Fasting

There are many reasons why a person can decide to seek the Lord's face in fasting.

For personal revival and spiritual awakening

David said: '*I humbled my soul with fasting*' (Psalm 35:13). This is needful in times of spiritual decline. These are times when we need to be revived. When you notice that your spirit is no longer enthusiastic about the things of God, or that you are losing your first love; when you are beginning to fall into sins and foolish mistakes you would not have fallen into in the past, or that you are losing the vision of the needy world; at such a time that you are not effective and fruitful in the service of the Lord, then you need a revival. The quickest and best way is to humble yourself before the Lord in sincere fasting and prayer, confess your sins and forsake your evil ways, and ask the Lord to revive and renew your strength and to anoint you again.

Charles G. Finney knew this. He said anytime he noticed a spiritual decline and that he was not being as fruitful and as effective as usual he would go aside to seek the face of the Lord in sincere prayer and fasting. This veteran soldier of the cross said that at no time did he fail to receive a re-awakening from the Lord. And he stirred up a great revival throughout his almost half-a-century of ministry, with much abiding fruit.

We need constant revival. We need to renew our strength often. That is the sure way to keep us from being weary and discouraged along the way. Yet there are many Christians in lukewarm states. They have lost their first zeal and love for the Lord. Such people should humble their souls with fasting. They should seek the Lord sincerely. Surely they shall be revived again. '*Blessed are they that mourn: for they shall be comforted*' Matthew 5:4; '*Humble yourselves in the sight of the Lord, and he shall lift you up*' (James 4:10).

To determine the perfect will of God

There are many vital decisions we have to make in life
– what job to take, where to live, who to marry and a
host of others which may or may not be equally weighty.
In all that we do in life, we should be satisfied with
nothing but the perfect will of God. All our petty desires
that are at variance with His, should be put aside.
We are to commit our ways to God and acknowledge
Him in all that we do. We are not to lean on our own
understanding at all. When we trust Him fully He leads
us in the path of righteousness for His name's sake –
we walk in His perfect will.

> *Trust in the Lord with all thine heart;*
> *And lean not unto thine own understanding.*
> *In all thy ways acknowledge him,*
> *And he shall direct thy paths.*
>
> (Proverbs 3:5–6)

Many times we come to crossroads, when we truly do
not know the perfect will of God for us. At such times
it is good to settle down and seek the face of the Lord
in sincere fasting and prayer. In the quietness of our
spirits we can receive direct leading from the Lord as
to where to go from there.

Often, at the beginning of an important task or a big
project, when one does not normally know what to do,
it is best to wait on the Lord in fasting.

Nehemiah received a report about the broken walls
of Jerusalem. He was burdened. But he did not rush to
do anything. He sat down, wept, fasted, prayed, and the
Lord led him aright. When Moses was to receive the
Law for the people of Israel, he was on a fast. When
Jesus, our Lord, was to begin His earthly ministry,

He fasted. There are many who are doubting whether or not the Lord wants them to go into the ministry and preach the Gospel. For clarity and understanding, settle down and seek the face of the Lord in fasting and prayer. He will lead you perfectly. *'The meek will he guide in judgment: And the meek will he teach his way'* (Psalm 25:9).

In 1977, two years after my conversion to Christ, I dedicated myself to serve the Lord in full-time ministry. I did not receive a call, I was only responding to the needs I saw around me. I was so burdened, seeing so many people unsaved, that I promised God that if He would use me, I would preach the Gospel full-time. However, in 1982, after my graduation from university, the call came clearly. The Lord began to speak to me about what He wanted me to do and how to do it. Now He was speaking clearly, asking me to abandon everything and go into the ministry full-time. Suddenly, the reality of the commitment I had made dawned on me. I saw what it takes to be a Gospel minister. I saw my utter inadequacies. It was so real, so, I told the Lord that I might not go again – and I meant it. I did not want to be a full-time Gospel minister, although I told Him I would still be preaching. Then I lost my peace. 'After all, it was I who first made a promise,' I said to myself. 'When the Lord gave me a call He did not say I should abandon my profession,' I continued. But my arguments did not settle the question. I, therefore, decided to fast and seek His face.

On one of those days the Lord spoke to me distinctly, and it is still fresh in my heart today. He told me that I should abandon everything and go into the field, giving me several promises and assurances if I would obey Him. Then He posed the question, 'Lovest thou Me more than these?' (my profession, members of my family who might disagree with me on my call, etc.). After a while, I gave Him an honest and sincere answer. Now, I strive each day to fulfil my commitment to the Lord and I am sure His grace will see me through until I lay down the sword at His feet.

At the same time He settled the case of who my beloved wife and co-labourer was going to be (an area in which I had almost made a serious mistake). When we seek the Lord sincerely in fasting and prayer, He makes clear His perfect will for our lives. *'And ye shall seek me, and find me, when ye shall search for me with all your heart'* (Jeremiah 29:13).

To move mountains and overcome crises

There are moments when you experience a crisis in your life – in the home, in your church or fellowship, or at work. The enemy then mounts an attack on you.

You may have prayed and exercised your faith without a solution. The devil may be threatening to scatter your home – where there is no harmony, there is no peace, it is devoid of love, joy and happiness, and it seems hopeless. It may be a demonic threat or oppression. It could even be an attack on your wife, children or relations. Take it up in earnest fasting and prayer and you will know real victory. It works!

In the work of the ministry we come across some tough cases – demonic possession, insanity, terrible and long-term sicknesses. The man of God may not fast on behalf of every individual, but the man of God who will successfully handle these situations to the glory of God has to be a man who regularly gives himself to fasting, ready for any emergency. Men who have been used of God (and those who are being used) have confessed to the fact that they find it very helpful taking time to fast and pray regularly and be alert spiritually

for any crisis situation. This is true of men such as
T. L. Osborn, Kenneth E. Hagin, Gordon Lindsay, A.
W. Tozer, Billy Graham and a host of others. When the
Lord was speaking about the fast that He has chosen,
He said:

> *Is not this the fast that I have chosen? to loose the*
> *bands of wickedness, to undo the heavy burdens,*
> *and to let the oppressed go free, and that ye break*
> *every yoke?*
>
> (Isaiah 58:6)

We should, therefore, fast to loose the bands of wickedness, to undo the heavy burden, to let the oppressed
go free, and to break every yoke.

To return a backslidden congregation to God

Sometimes the state of a congregation of the people of
God is such that it demands very serious attention.
Perhaps they have gone deep into disobedience, sin
and rebellion, worldliness and carelessness, such that
they no longer show forth the glory of God. A fast can
be proclaimed and a solemn assembly called, that the
people may seek the face of the Lord. This happened
when Nehemiah and Ezra were leaders of the people
of Israel. The children of Israel had departed from the
law of God. They had begun to take foreign wives. They
were desecrating the sabbath. Princes and leaders were
the ring leaders. Ezra heard it, he wept, fasted, prayed
and called the elders together. Eventually a solemn
assembly was called and the people returned to God.

There is a need for such an assembly today. Many
churches have backslidden. Many congregations have
gone astray. There is hardly any distinction between
the people of God and the people of the world in many

Christian assemblies. The fruit of the Spirit is terribly lacking among the people of God and there is too much love for things of the world. Many are unequally yoked with unbelievers in unholy wedlock and business alliances. Many assemblies are dead, although they still appear to be alive. Many have lost their first love, yet are full of various activities. To some ministers this is normal, because we are in the last days, while many other ministers of the Gospel are totally blind to this terrible lukewarm state of the Church. I am not trying to be censorious; I am, I hope, only speaking the mind of God.

> *Cry aloud, spare not, lift up thy voice like a trumpet, and shew my people their transgression, and the house of Jacob their sins.*
>
> (Isaiah 58:1)

> . . . Hath this been in your days, or even in the days of your fathers? . . .
> Sanctify ye a fast, call a solemn assembly, gather the elders and all the inhabitants of the land into the house of the LORD your God, and cry unto the LORD.
> Blow ye the trumpet in Zion, and sound an alarm in my holy mountain: let all the inhabitants of the land tremble: for the day of the LORD cometh, for it is nigh at hand; . . .
>
> (Joel 1:2; 1:14; 2:1)

When we see a congregation degenerating like this, it is profitable to proclaim a fast during which the leader will lead the people back to God in genuine repentance and humility. I have seen it work in quite a number of assemblies. It will still work for us today.

Fasting to avert national calamity and disaster

When the children of Israel were in exile they faced a genuine threat of total annihilation. The devil wanted to wipe the God-chosen people off the face of the earth. You would have expected an automatic response from God. But God works through men. When men do not make themselves available, His hands are tied. When Esther, through her uncle, Mordecai, knew of the devil's plot, she proclaimed a fast for her maids and all the children of Israel for three days and three nights. God then intervened and delivered Israel, and destroyed her enemies. (This account is found in the book of Esther.)

In II Chronicles 20, three nations besieged the land of Judah. They were definitely the more powerful. Jehoshaphat the king proclaimed a fast. While they were praying, the Lord spoke to them in a prophecy. They acted according to the Word of the Lord and won the victory. The three nations fought and destroyed one another and the nation of Judah was miraculously delivered.

Nineveh was such a wicked city, that the Lord decided to overthrow it in forty days. He sent His prophet to them. *'Yet forty days, and Nineveh shall be overthrown'* (Jonah 3:4). So the king commanded all the inhabitants to fast and turn to the Lord, and the Lord had mercy and spared Nineveh. A lot of national catastrophes could be averted if the people of God would humble themselves and seek the face of the Lord in fasting. America once did it and got results. Britain also did it. We have done it in the past in Nigeria, and God was faithful to His Word in answering our prayers. We can still do it today in sincerity and truth, and we shall discover that the Lord is ever faithful to

His Word. He will send mercy and blessings in reponse to genuine national repentance and prayer.

> *If my people, which are called by name, shall humble themselves, and turn from their wicked ways; then will I hear from heaven and will forgive their sin, and will heal their land.*
>
> (II Chronicles 7:14)

We have witnessed and taken part in many national prayer and intercession camps, where people of God genuinely sought God's face for Nigeria, and fasted for days. We praise the Lord for mighty deliverances He has wrought through these meetings. But, may the day come when the government of my nation shall call on all her citizens to fast and pray for the nation.

We can also fast to receive revelation from the Lord as Daniel and Moses did. We can fast so that the work of the Lord may prosper in our hands like the apostle Paul. We can also fast to worship and minister to the Lord. In all our fasting, however, we should have a clear understanding of one thing: fasting in itself does not have power. Power belongs to God. But fasting brings us to a state where our spirits are broken and contrite, which God cannot despise, and our faith is strong and active and thereby we can easily receive from the Lord, and tap from His infinite power. Biblical fasting, therefore, releases the power of God to work in our situation.

Types Of Fast

There are three major types of fast spoken of in Scripture.

The absolute fast

This is when you do not eat any food or drink any water for some days. It could be one, two, or three days. Apart from Moses, who was with God on Mount Horeb twice for forty days and forty nights without eating or drinking there is no other record in the Scriptures of an absolute fast exceeding three days. And medical advice is that three days is the maximum to go without food and water, without causing damage to our bodies. An absolute fast is required only when the case in consideration is very important and urgent.

Esther fasted for three days and three nights, without food or drink, because there was an urgent decree to destroy all Israelites (Esther 4:16). Saul fasted for three days in this way because he had a unique encounter with the Lord on his way to Damascus (Acts 9:9). Therefore, it is not common to embark on an absolute fast unless the case is very important and urgent and we are led by the Lord to do so. And when this occurs it should not exceed three days.

A minister of the Gospel returned from the field one day to find his wife, whom he had left perfectly well and healthy, totally deaf and dumb. Despite all that he tried nothing happened. At the leading of the Lord he began a three-day, absolute fast. At the end of it he cast out a demon he had previously dealt with on the mission field, that had come to afflict his wife. There is need for Gospel ministers (and husbands of course) to protect their homes from demonic assaults.

The long fast

This is when you have to seek the face of the Lord for a long period of time. It would range from three days to one week, two weeks, three weeks, or even forty days. During the period you do not eat any food but you take

plenty of clean water to both purge your system and
keep the body organs from collapsing. This fast can be
as long as the Lord leads you, but it is advisable not to
be longer than forty days. This is for a normal healthy
person.

This appears to be the type of fast our Lord Jesus
did. Immediately after the fast the Bible says He was
hungry.

*And when he had fasted forty days and forty
nights, he was afterward an hungered.*
(Matthew 4:2)

Normally, when you abstain from food and water over
a long period of time, it is not the hunger pangs that
return first. You are, first and foremost, thirsty and you
want to drink something. That Jesus was not thirsty
here but hungry is quite suggestive. People can fast for
one, two, three, seven or more days taking nothing but
water. But during the time of fasting you spend a lot of
time in prayer and in the Word.

The partial fast
This is the type that Daniel practised when he was
seeking the face of the Lord concerning Israel.

*In those days I Daniel was mourning three full
weeks. I ate no pleasant bread, neither came flesh
nor wine in my mouth, neither did I anoint myself
at all, till three whole weeks were fulfilled.*
(Daniel 10:2–3)

In this instance he did not undertake a normal fast.
This could be because of the heavy demand of his duty
or some other unexplained reasons. He resorted to a

partial fast. He did not eat any fancy food, no meat, no wine but simple, light food. It is on record that John Wesley practised this type of fasting, living on dry bread and water for a period of time whilst seeking the face of God. Gordon Lindsay said: 'Not everyone seems to be able to enter into a total fast. Personally, we have found fruit juice fasts nearly as effective as the total fast.'

With these three types of fast, the fasting can be personal, or collective – congregational or national. It can also be voluntary or imposed, depending on the situation. It can be regular or occasional. But it is very good if a Christian can have a regular day of prayer and fasting.

How To Fast

To help you in this spiritual exercise, we want to give some useful hints.

Firstly, you can fast, but the devil will not want you to make any attempt to use this weapon against him. 'You have never done it before' he may say, Yes, but you are starting now. 'You will be very hungry.' Well, it is also good for personal discipline. If you fast you will be hungry but you won't die in the process; rather you cultivate self-control which is a fruit of the Spirit. 'What about your health?' The Lord will keep you strong and healthy. Even if you have a disease that can necessitate an excuse, the Lord can heal you if you believe Him for it. 'Do it another time,' he may suggest. The devil has used these excuses against many who wanted to begin a fast. I normally tell the devil I will not put it off. The time is now. Live moment by moment and do not think of the seemingly long time the fast will take. Moment by moment, by faith, and soon the whole exercise is successfully completed. Do not allow the devil to hinder you by tempting you to think you cannot fast. If you can miss your morning meal, then you can miss the afternoon meal also. If you can fast for one day then you can fast for more days. Just live moment by moment until the deed is done and the victory is won.

Secondly, do not fast just for fasting's sake, but have a particular purpose in mind, Define your goal. Is it for the nation? Is it to move a mountain in your life or in another person's life? Is it to request a particular cherished desire of your heart? Decide and be specific. Keep your heart on the Lord and let Him meet you on the subject of your desire. Do not allow other things to distract your attention. Be single-minded and let your prayers be intense for that particular goal. And you shall have what you desire. (Mark 11:24).

During periods of fasting, create much time to study the Word of God and to pray. You can arrange your fasting for such a time that will enable you to study the Word and pray. Although fasting itself is a spiritual worship to God if rightly done, yet you get the most out of it when you have time for the Word of God and for prayer. This is very important.

Keep the principles of spiritual discipline when fasting. As much as possible *'Let not thy left hand know what thy right hand doeth'* (Mattew 6:3).

I do not think there is any work that a normal, healthy person can do that can hinder or be hindered by a one-day fast. But if the fast is to be lengthy, make sure it does not interfere with your job. You should make proper arrangements so that your job is in no way jeopardised. As a believer, you ought to have a good testimony at work.

When you fast, it is not advisable to break it with solid food if it is longer than a day. This could harm your already-sensitised and relaxed alimentary canal. When you begin a fast, be disciplined enough to finish it. Do not break it prematurely.

Fasting – Use It But Don't Abuse It

Fasting is a very effective weapon of war that we have; let us use it but not abuse it.

Many people think that they cannot receive anything from God, or hear anything from Him, or receive direction or leading until they have fasted. This is wrong. If you have faith, all things are possible. Fasting only helps to strengthen your faith, sensitise your spirit, and allow you to settle down to proper praying and listening to God.

Some practise a regular fasting once or twice a week, or once in two weeks. This is a very useful spiritual exercise. But do not become enslaved to fasting. For example if you have decided to fast every Wednesday, there may be something that necessitates your changing it to another time. Fasting is made for you and not you for fasting. Be flexible in the hand of the Holy Spirit. We should allow for occasional providential over-ruling of God, in the practice of fasting I hope you understand this teaching.

Some people fast continuously without any specific purpose. Some demons can get people into bondage in this manner. Apart from your regular fasting period, whenever it occurs to you to fast for more than one day, check what the purpose is and see if it stands the test of the Word of God. You can pray for the Lord to lead you in it.

Many people will want to bribe God with fasting. They are living in sin and disobedience. They are not willing to repent of their sins and turn to the Lord. Yet they fast for one thing or the other. It is a barren and wasted exercise. Unless you have repented of your sin and you are living right before God, you are merely starving yourself of food. Some fast so that their so-called enemies (human beings) may be destroyed. This is especially practised in a lot of white-garment churches in Africa. This is wrong. This happened to the people of Israel. The Lord said to them:

> *Behold, in the day of your fast ye find pleasure, and exact all your labours. Behold, ye fast for strife and debate, and to smite with the fist of wickedness: ye shall not fast as ye do this day, to make your voice to be heard on high.*
>
> (Isaiah 58:3—4).

The Lord then told them to repent of their sins and be just and righteous, and fast with the right motive. Then they would be heard on high. This applies to you also. Obedience is better than sacrifice. Repent. Plead the blood of Jesus. Set your heart in order before the Lord. Turn from your wicked ways. Then you can fast and you will have the blessings that follow fasting.

Great Blessings From Fasting

Apart from the fact that you will have what you desire from the Lord, He has additional blessings to bestow on you when you fast in His appointed way. These blessings are spiritual, physical and material.

*Then shall thy light break forth as the morning,
and thine health shall spring forth speedily: and
thy righteousness shall go before thee; the glory of
the LORD shall be thy rereward.*

*Then shalt thou call, and the LORD shall answer;
thou shalt cry, and he shall say, Here I am.
If thou take away from the midst of thee the
yoke, the putting forth of the finger, and speaking
vanity; and if thou draw out thy soul to the
hungry, and satisfy the afflicted soul; then shall
thy light rise in obscurity, and thy darkness be
as the noonday: and the LORD shall give thee,
and satisfy thy soul in drought, and make fat
thy bones: and thou shalt be like a watered
garden, and like a spring of water, whose waters
fail not.*

*And they that shall be of thee shall build the old
waste places: thou shalt raise up the foundations
of many generations; and thou shalt be called,
The repairer of the breach, The restorer of paths
to dwell in.*

(Isaiah 58:8–12)

These promises are great inded. We can find at least
ten:

(1) Your light will shine.
(2) Your righteousness will show.
(3) Your health shall blossom.
(4) The glory of God shall overshadow you.
(5) The Lord will give you speedy answers to prayers.
(6) You will enjoy continous divine guidance.
(7) You will have satisfaction even at a time of general
    lack. You will be like a well-watered garden.

(8) You will experience constant refreshing from the Lord.

(9) Your work and spiritual ministrations will produce lasting fruits and eternal results.

(10) You will bring about revival and restoration to others.

If anything is worth doing at all, fasting unto the Lord is really worth doing. You should begin to take advantage of this mighty weapon of war today.

Chapter Eleven

By The Anointing

The anointing of the Holy Spirit is an indispensable weapon in spiritual warfare. This is the unction of the Holy One, the power of the Holy Spirit resting upon a Christian. No one can fight effectively and prevail without the power of the Holy Spirit operating in his or her life.

A great number of Christians are ignorant of this fact. The reason why many fail and suffer defeat so often is that they lack the power of the Spirit of God in their lives. Even amongst ministers of the Gospel, many labour and strive in their own efforts to promote the Kingdom of God. Without the power of the Spirit of God, spiritual labours end up in fruitlessness, frustration and exhaustion.

A picture of this is given in the lives of the sons of the prophet in the time of Elisha (II Kings 6:1–7). The place where they were living was too small for them. They went to cut wood for beams for a bigger place. While they were working, the axe-head fell into the water. They were left with just the stick. Not only was it borrowed but how many beams could they cut without it? And how many Christians today attempt to do the work of the Lord without 'the axe head' – the power of the Holy Spirit? How many have even lost the power and the anointing and are just struggling to go on? For a victorious Christian life, for effective and fruitful Christian service, for victory in spiritual warfare, you need the power of the Holy Spirit. It is indispensable.

The devil does not respect your age and experience if you lack the power of God. He does not respect your eloquence or profound knowledge of the Scriptures if the power of God is not in your life. Satan recognises, respects and gives way only to the anointing of the Holy Spirit. It is the anointing alone that breaks the yoke. It is the anointing alone that puts the devil to flight.

The Anointing Makes The Difference

The anointing of the Holy Spirit will make a lot of difference in your life. I have observed very definitely how the anointing makes certain people different among the people of God. What makes some people pray so hard, so fervently, so long, over a problem without any solution and yet some pray for a few seconds and there is a definite answer.

What makes a man of God give a very simple Gospel message to a crowd and people come streaming to the altar with tears on their faces, accepting Jesus as Lord? No coercion, no shouting, no harassment, no profound theology, yet the people respond and are genuinely saved. Or what makes a man teach the Word of God, and the Word just keeps moving like a living force inside you, pure and strong, and inspiring you to take some definite steps? What makes a man come to a meeting and it is as though the thoughts of his heart are revealed in the message? What really happens when a long-standing problem suddenly gives way because a man just offered some earnest prayer?

It is the anointing that breaks the yoke. When you are under the anointing of the Holy Spirit, the power of God will flow through you effortlessly, problems will be solved, needs will be met and people's lives will be refreshed.

For a life that will be a blessing to others, for effective service and ministry you must have the anointing of the Lord upon your life.

This is not just for preachers or ministers of the Gospel alone. Every Christian is a witness for Jesus. We have all received the ministry of reconciliation. But can we ever be fruitful without the power of the Holy Spirit? Impossible. Even Jesus our Lord could not operate and bless others until He received the power of the Holy Spirit. And when He was going He charged all His disciples to wait for the power before they went out to witness to the world. *'And, behold, I send the promise of my Father upon you: but tarry ye in the city of Jerusalem, until ye be endued with power from on high'* (Luke 24:49).

Endued with power from on high! That was exactly what they needed to overcome the hostile forces of darkness and proclaim triumphantly the message of the redeeming Christ.

Today, we do not need to wait. The Holy Spirit is here now. Divine power and anointing are now available for whoever wants them – Alleluia! And the anointing will make the whole difference in your life.

Samuel, the prophet, said to Saul, when he was to become Israel's first king:

And the Spirit of the LORD will come upon thee, and thou shalt prophesy with them, and shalt be turned into another man.

(I Samuel 10:6)

This is to say, the Spirit of the Almighty shall come upon you to mark you different from the multitude and transform your life completely. The coming of the anointing will bring a complete transformation in your life.

I remember the time the Lord graciously visited me with His anointing. For some time before then, I had been longing deeply for the power of the Holy Spirit to enable me to serve Him effectively. That night the Lord blessed me and I knew it. My whole life underwent a deep revolution. My understanding of the Word of God became clearer; my prayer life was deepened; I could minister more effectively. We need to be renewed and deepened in our spiritual experiences daily. When the anointing of the Lord comes upon you it will be obvious. You are transformed into another man, a Spirit-filled, Spirit-controlled man.

Victory By The Anointing

It is by the anointing of the Holy Spirit that we overcome the devil and his hosts. *'Not by might, nor by power, but by my spirit, saith the LORD of hosts'* (Zechariah 4:6). Satan is a spiritual being with a measure of supernatural power. Likewise, his demons and evil spirits. No human being can overcome them alone in the flesh.

It is as the anointing of the Lord comes upon us that we prevail against the devil. If you are under the anointing of the Holy Spirit your victory over Satan is sure and certain. It is rather like Samson. Whenever the anointing was not upon him he was an ordinary man. But with the anointing on him, then the supernatural power of God would be in operation and nothing would be impossible to him. Once he came upon a hungry lion which roared at him – merely seeing a hungry lion in the zoo is fearsome – but for the anointing, Samson was a sure prey. But, *'the Spirit of the Lord came mightily upon him, and he rent him as he would have rent a kid, and he had nothing in his hand'* (Judges 14:6). How many times the devil roars like a lion, wanting to devour the people of God. Like Samson, when the anointing comes upon us, we will tear the lion into pieces instead of being his prey. To deal effectively with Satan the anointing of the Spirit is indispensable.

Another time, Samson slew one thousand Philistines. He had been captured and bound with strong new cords. Three thousand hefty men surrounded him – there was no chance to escape or survive. When his captors shouted at him, the anointing of the Holy Spirit came mightily upon him. His fetters were broken and he killed a thousand men with a mere jawbone of an ass.

> *And when he came unto Lehi, the Philistines shouted against him: and the Spirit of the LORD came mightily upon him, and the cords that were upon his arms became as flax that was burnt with fire, and his bands loosed from off his hands. And he found a new jawbone of an ass, and put forth his hand, and took it, and slew a thousand men therewith.*
>
> (Judges 15:14–15)

How every cord will break when the anointing comes! Simple materials, gifts, talents that could be considered nothing can become mighty weapons of deliverance and victory as the power of the Holy Spirit rests upon you. A jawbone of an ass became the weapon of victory.

Likewise, the rod of Moses became a rod of deliverance, just because of the anointing of the Holy Spirit. When the power of God rests upon you, a simple touch of faith releases tremendous power. A simple testimony or witnessing brings people unto the Lord. We need to come and abide under the anointing of the Spirit of the Lord. That is the way to fight spiritual battles in these days.

David was another man who operated under the anointing of the Holy Spirit. On three different occasions the Lord gave him a strong anointing of the Holy Spirit. When he was a young boy the Lord saw that his heart was perfect towards Him. David had a deep yearning for God – a heart after God. Seeing his sincerity, the Lord anointed him to be the king of Israel.

> *Then Samuel took the horn of oil, and anointed him in the midst of his brethren: and the Spirit of the LORD came upon David from that day forward.*
>
> (I Samuel 16:13)

At two other different occasions he was anointed.

> *And the men of Judah came, and there they anointed David king over the house of Judah.*
>
> (II Samuel 2:4)

> *So all the elders of Israel came to the king to Hebron; and king David made a league with them in Hebron before the LORD: and they anointed David king over Israel.*
>
> (II Samuel 5:3)

David did exploits in the strength of this anointing. The majority of the inspirational and prophetic psalms we

have in the Bible today came from him as he operated
under the anointing. All the battles he fought were in
the strength of the Lord. He could say,

> *Some trust in chariots, and some in horses:*
> *But we will remember the name of the LORD*
> *   our God.*
> *They are brought down and fallen:*
> *But we are risen, and stand upright.*
>
> (Psalm 20:7–8)

Do you think David could have killed Goliath in his
own strength? There was not a chance in a million that
this could ever happen. Humanly speaking Goliath was
a mighty warrior, David was just a lad. Goliath was
armed to the teeth, David had only a strong faith, five
stones, and a shepherd's staff. But David was not just
operating in the physical. The anointing of the Holy
Spirit was upon him and that divine power brought
Goliath tumbling down. The power of the Spirit of God
in your life can defeat every 'Goliath' permanently.
Victory does not come by strength or human efforts.
It comes by the power and anointing of the Spirit
of God.

Spiritual Gifts By The Anointing

The gifts of the Spirit will fully manifest under the
anointing. There are spiritual gifts meant for believers.
They are for us today. God does not want us to be ignorant, but to be conversant with and take advantage of
them. The Bible says: *'Now concerning spiritual gifts,
brethren, I would not have you ignorant* (I Corinthians
12:1).

The gifts are for us to profit by, by bringing an increase to the Kingdom of God. *'But the manifestation of the Spirit is given to every man to profit withal'* (I Corinthians 12:7).

The gifts are for us to fight a good spiritual warfare.

> *This charge I commit unto thee, son Timothy, according to the prophecies which went before on thee, that thou by them [by the prophecies] mightest war a good warfare.*
>
> (I Timothy 1:18)

The Church will wax ever stronger if believers are greatly edified, and unbelievers converted in great multitudes, as we take advantage of the gifts of the Spirit. You have the right to the gifts of the Holy Spirit; but they operate under the anointing of the Holy Spirit. As the anointing and the power of the Holy Spirit comes upon you, the gifts manifest fully. Seek the anointing today. *'Seek the LORD, and his strength: Seek his face ever more'* (Psalm 105:4).

It is not only the gifts of the Holy Spirit that are manifested in the life of an anointed man; by the anointing also comes the grace of the Spirit. This is the manifestations of the fruit of the Spirit which are so vital in order to maintain a sound Christian testimony and to live a life acceptable to God and His people. The fruit of the Spirit is so vital to you as a Christian, forming the protective covering against all the assaults of the devil, and constituting the armour of God – Ephesians 6:10–18. And it is not sufficient to have sophisticated weapons without any armour. You must have the protective coverings of the Holy Spirit.

This is why the Bible says that there is no law against them.

But the fruit of the Spirit is love, joy, peace, long-suffering, gentleness, goodness, faith, meekness, temperance: against such there is no law.
                                        (Galatians 5:22–23)

These are so effective in disarming Satan. Remember, Jesus as the Lamb of God dealt with Satan, and the devil could not overcome Him. By being filled with the anointing, these manifestations come upon your life and by them you disarm the devil completely.

Luis Palau, a world-renowned evangelist, in explaining this scripture, *'against such there is no law'* asked:

Do you know what that means? 'Against such there is no law.' It means that there is no law against loving too much. God will never come alongside of you and say, 'You've loved enough, better put on the brakes awhile.' There is no law against love.

Likewise there is no law against too much joy. You can never be too joyful in Jesus Christ. God is never going to say, 'You've had enough fun for a while. Now I'm going to cool it for you.' The Lord says *'rejoice always'*.

The same goes for peace. You cannot have too much of it. Our Lord even promised us perfect peace in the midst of the turbulence of life. You cannot be too gentle, too good, too faithful, too meek. Your self-control cannot be too much, you are to have these manifestations of the fruit of the Spirit in abundance.

It is however very important to note, nothing else matters if you do not manifest the fruit of the Spirit in your life. For example, without love, all the other manifestations of the Spirit in your life do not really matter. The apostle Paul used a whole chapter in Scripture to prove that – I Corinthians 13. Hence we must have the fruit of the Spirit as well as the gifts of the Spirit. When you are truly anointed of the Lord, these manifestations will flow copiously.

Ministering Effectively

Human problems are so complex that it takes the power of God to deal with them thoroughly. It is by the anointing that we are able to minister to people effectively and get their needs met. When the anointing of the Lord is upon you, Satan is forced to withdraw from the life of whosoever you are ministering to. That is one of the key reasons God makes His anointing available to us – to enable us to minister effectively to others and make them disciples of Jesus. Even Jesus Christ our Lord could minister effectively to the needs of men only because He was anointed of the Spirit.

The Spirit of the LORD is upon me,
Because he hath anointed me to preach the
gospel to the poor;
He hath sent me to heal the brokenhearted, to
preach deliverance to the captives,
And recovering of sight to the blind,
To set at liberty them that are bruised.

(Luke 4:18)

How God anointed Jesus of Nazareth with the
Holy Ghost and with power: who went about
doing good, and healing all that were oppressed
of the devil; for God was with him

(Acts 10:38)

With the anointing of the Spirit of God, we are able to break every hold of Satan on any of his victims, we are able to minister effectively to their total needs – spirit, soul and body. There is no fruitless ministration if you are under the anointing. The devil cannot resist you. It is the Lord now at work in you, dealing with Satan and liberating the sons of men. This is the cardinal reason for which God anoints us with the Holy Spirit – to make us effective witnesses of the Gospel message and of His resurrection power.

> *But ye shall receive power, after that the Holy Ghost is come upon you: and ye shall be witnesses unto me both in Jerusalem, and in all Judaea, and in Samaria, and unto the uttermost part of the earth.*
>
> (Acts 1:8)

> *And we are his witnesses of these things; and so is also the Holy Ghost, whom God hath given to them that obey him.*
>
> (Acts 5:32)

If, therefore, you seek to be greatly anointed of the Holy Spirit for the purpose of ministering effectively to men, bringing them into the Kingdom of God, the Lord will surely visit and anoint you.

To Be Used Of God

When God wants to use certain people for some special tasks, He first gives them a great anointing of the Holy Spirit. It is the anointing that qualifies them for His service, following the period of severe preparations.

It has been like that right from the Old Testament.
Moses, Joshua, Samuel, Elijah, Daniel and all the
prophets were greatly anointed with the Holy Spirit.
It was so in the New Testament too. But there is a
great difference.

In the Old Testament time, there were only three
categories of people that could be anointed with the
Holy Spirit – the prophet, the priest, and the king.
In the time of national emergencies, God would anoint
some people to deliver Israel but the whole nation could
not enjoy the anointing.

Now it is quite different. Although there are people
who are called and set apart in the body of Christ as
leaders with ministry-anointing, yet all that believe on
the Lord Jesus as their Saviour and Lord can now enjoy
the full anointing of the Holy Spirit. The Bible says,

> For the promise is unto you, and to your children,
> and to all that are afar off, even as many as the
> Lord our God shall call.

> (Acts 2:39)

If you have heard and responded to the call of the Lord
then the power of the Holy Spirit is available to you.

How To Receive The Anointing

To receive the fullness of this anointing, therefore, the
following should be borne in mind.

First, you must be sure that you have been born
again, that you have received Christ by faith into
your heart. This is not negotiable. Jesus said that
the people of the world that have not been born again
cannot receive the Holy Spirit.

Even the Spirit of truth; whom the world cannot receive, because it seeth him not, neither knoweth him: but ye know him; for he dwelleth with you, and shall be in you.

(John 14:17)

A man once came forward to receive the power of the Holy Spirit in one of our meetings. Everyone else received the power but although he prayed for a long time he really did not receive anything. I was bothered. And then the Holy Spirit told me clearly that the man had not been born again and that he also needed deliverance from some demonic afflictions. He confirmed this. We first led him to repent and accept Christ as his Lord and Saviour. Then we ministered deliverance to him. Immediately, the power of the Holy Spirit fell upon him and he spoke in tongues. You must first be born again. The Bible says,

Repent, and be baptized every one of you in the name of Jesus Christ for the remission of sins, and ye shall receive the gift of the Holy Ghost.

(Acts 2:38)

Secondly, the power of the Holy Spirit is available to the man or woman who is ready to consecrate his or her entire life to God and obey Him all the way. We have not been emphasising this crucial point enough in the Church. The Bible says,

And we are his witnesses of these things; and so is also the Holy Ghost, whom God hath given to them that obey him.

(Acts 5:32)

Do you know the reason why Jesus Christ had such tremendous anointing of the Spirit operating in His life? The Bible gives the answer.

> *Thou hast loved righteousness, and hated iniquity;*
> *Therefore God, even thy God, hath anointed thee*
> *With the oil of gladness above thy fellows.*
>
> (Hebrews 1:9)

Please take note of that one word, 'Therefore'. It implies that He had a tremendous anointing of the Spirit because He was perfectly consecrated to God. Those who are pure can understand best the mind and revelation of God and can operate easily in the anointing of the Holy Spirit. The anointing of the Lord will come upon a ready vessel; a willing vessel, purged of all uncleanness and living for God.

Thirdly, the anointing of the Lord will come upon the person that has a strong desire for it. The Bible says, '*Deep calleth unto deep*' (Psalm 42:7). The deeper your desire the easier for the anointing to come.

> *For I will pour water upon him that is thirsty,*
> *and floods upon the dry ground: I will pour my*
> *spirit upon thy seed, and my blessing upon thine*
> *offspring.*
>
> (Isaiah 44:3)

Elijah was a great man of God. He would pray and fire would fall from heaven, and the barren give birth. He raised the dead and did many other mighty things in the power of the Spirit of God. He said to Elisha his servant, '*Ask what I shall do for thee, before I be taken away from thee*' (II Kings 2:9). Elisha could have asked for money, clothes, properties or many other things that were within the ability of Elijah to give him. But his heart's desire was so strong, he asked for nothing but a double portion of the anointing on Elijah.

> *I pray thee, let a double portion of thy spirit be upon me. And he [Elijah] said, Thou hast asked a hard thing: nevertheless, if thou see me when I am taken from thee, it shall be so unto thee; but if not, it shall not be so.*
>
> (II Kings 2:9–10)

You can see that receiving the anointing is conditional. And if the pronouncements of Elijah could come true, One greater than Elijah has promised to give you power. Let your desire be strong, and He will surely anoint you with the Holy Spirit and with power.

Fourthly, the anointing of the Lord will come upon the person that asks from God. We must ask in faith. We must ask expectantly. It is as we ask that we receive. God has a lot to give if we would only ask. You can ask for the anointing of the Holy Spirit upon your life and ministry today.

> *And I say unto you, Ask, and it shall be given you; seek, and ye shall find; knock, and it shall be opened unto you. For every one that asketh receiveth; and he that seeketh findeth; and to him that knocketh it shall be opened. If a son shall ask bread of any of you that is a father, will he give him a stone? or if he ask a fish, will he for a fish give him a serpent? Or if he shall ask an egg, will he offer him a scorpion? If ye then, being evil, know how to give good gifts unto your children: how much more shall your heavenly Father give the Holy Spirit to them that ask him?*
>
> (Luke 11:9–13)

Operating In The Anointing

No, it is not sufficient to be anointed in the Holy Spirit; you have to take advantage of the anointing. You are to stop struggling. You simply trust the Holy Spirit, co-operate with Him and let the anointing flow.

In times of prayer, you know that left alone you cannot pray effectively and powerfully. Hence, you consciously ask the Holy Spirit to inspire, lead, guide and energise you so you can pray effectively.

> *Likewise the Spirit also helpeth our infirmities: for we know not what we should pray for as we ought: but the Spirit itself maketh intercession for us with groanings which cannot be uttered. And he that searcheth the hearts knoweth what is the mind of the Spirit, because he maketh intercession for the saints according to the will of God.*
>
> (Romans 8:26–27)

Likewise in your study of the Scriptures, you realise that the carnal Christian mind cannot understand the things of God; that it takes the Holy Spirit, the Author of the Sacred Volume, to understand the deep meaning of the Word. You simply let the anointing flow and the Spirit teaches you.

> *But the Comforter, which is the Holy Ghost, whom the Father will send in my name, he shall teach you all things, and bring all things to your remembrance, whatsoever I have said unto you.*
>
> (John 14:26)

When you are sharing the Gospel with people, you simply trust the Holy Spirit who knows the depth of the

hearts of men to lead you to the scriptures you will use
to meet the need of such people and lead them to Christ.
When you are being persecuted for righteousness' sake
or you are being called to question on the preaching of
the Gospel, only trust the Holy Spirit to take control
and give you the appropriate words.

> *But when they deliver you up, take no thought
> how or what ye shall speak: for it shall be given
> you in that same hour what ye shall speak. For it
> is not ye that speak, but the Spirit of your Father
> which speaketh in you.*
>
> (Matthew 10:19–20)

Stephen experienced this, he was so full of the power
of the Holy Spirit that *'they were not able to resist
the wisdom and the spirit by which he spake'* (Acts
6:10). This is exactly how to operate in the anointing
of God.

When you are ministering deliverance to people,
knowing that it is the anointing that breaks every
yoke, you allow the anointing to flow. Walking in
the Spirit, being led by the Spirit, ministering under
the anointing, you find your whole life so rich and so
fruitful for God.

Today, as you read this chapter, something glorious
will happen to you. Trust the Lord right now for a new
anointing. Ask in faith. He will give you that which will
make you a terrible menance to Satan and his hosts.
You will be able to fight in the strength of the Lord.

Receive ye the Holy Ghost.

(John 20:22)

Chapter Twelve

Boldness As A Weapon Of War

Have not I commanded thee? Be strong and of a good courage; be not afraid, neither be thou dismayed: for the LORD thy God is with thee withersoever thou goest.

(Joshua 1:9)

B oldness is a crucial weapon in spiritual warfare. If you will defeat the enemy, then you must be bold, you must be strong. You cannot afford to be weak and fearful. Weakness will make you vulnerable.

Boldness is not something that comes naturally. It has to be developed. What comes naturally is fear and a sense of weakness and unworthiness. All of God's giants started out with fear. Then God spoke courage into them. They responded in faith and went forth to do great things. Moses was fearful when God called to him in the burning bush. He was scared of having to go back to confront Pharaoh from whom he had fled sometime before. Gideon was filled with a sense of unworthiness – then God addressed him as a mighty man of valour. For a long time he had been part of an oppressed nation with a slave mentality. Jeremiah felt too small for the task God called him to do. He felt he was too young to confront a sinning Israel with the Word of the Lord, just as Joshua felt inadequate when he had to step into Moses' shoes. He had seen God perform extraordinary things through Moses; he had seen the awful level of rebelliousness of the people. He felt he could not cope. In all these cases however, when God spoke and encouraged these men, they took on boldness as a weapon of war and went ahead to accomplish the divine purpose for their lives. It does not matter what task or situation you face.

It does not matter how you presently feel about yourself or about the assignment God has given you. It does not really matter what has happened in the past or what is happening to you presently. Be bold. Be strong. Rise up in faith and courage; take your weapons of war. The Lord is with you and He will give you complete victory over the adversary. What is important now is not what happened to you in the past. The crucial issue now is whether or not you will receive boldness from God today and go forth and affect your generation for God.

Fear Not

There is a phrase that occurs over and over again in the Scriptures. It is 'fear not'. God does not want us to live in fear. He wants us to be totally free from it. There is nobody living in fear that can be an effective soldier of the cross. The spirit of fear must be dealt with in your life today.

Certain things are made clear in the Scriptures about fear:

- Fear is not from God. God has not given us the spirit of fear, but of power, of love and of a sound mind (II Timothy 1:7).

- There is a spirit of fear, hence fear is not ordinary. It is a demon that must be cast out (Romans 8:15).
- Fear has torment. The people living in fear experience constant torments, oppressions and depression. (I John 4:18).
- Fear brings bondage. A man living in fear is made subject to bondage. You are not really free in your spirit. You are not enjoying the glorious liberty of the sons of God. Fear binds (Hebrews 2:14–15).
- Fear is the greatest enemy of faith. Faith is a formidable weapon of spiritual warfare, but fear weakens and destroys this all-important weapon. Fear and faith cannot grow together (Mark 4:20).
- Fear is a weapon of affliction of Satan. Whenever the enemy really wants to deal with someone he sends fear first. When fear strikes, it opens the door for the other agents of Satan to come in to afflict. You must not open your life to fear.
- Fear will limit your possibilities in God. Because of fear people have all manner of reasons why they are not making progress. So long as fear is accommodated there will always be an excuse for failure.

These are some of the reasons why God says in His Word repeatedly, 'Fear not', 'Be not afraid', 'Be not dismayed'.

Fear thou not; for I am with thee: be not dismayed; for I am thy God: I will strengthen thee; yea, I will

help thee; yea, I will uphold thee with the right
hand of my righteousness.

(Isaiah 41:10)

Be Bold, Be Strong

There is the need to move from the negative – fear –
to the positive – faith and boldness. It is not sufficient
simply not to be afraid. You have to be bold and be
strong in the Lord. In his writing to the Ephesian
church, on spiritual warfare, Paul commanded, *'Be*
strong in the Lord, and in the power of His might'.
He was addressing the subject of divine boldness. One
of the critically needed virtues for Christians these
days is boldness. There are too many compromisers.
There are too many deserters in the army of the Lord.
We fear persecutions. We are too concerned about our
reputation, hence we are not prepared to take any risk.
We have removed the dividing line between the world
and the Church. What an unholy wedlock! We do not
categorically speak out against sin and social injustice.
We water down God's Word and do not speak it as it is.
Many believers no longer openly witness and preach the
Gospel to others. We are anaemic, rather than dynamic.
What is lacking? Boldness. The kind that Elijah had
which enabled him to confront wicked Ahab and the
prophet of Baal; the kind that John the Baptist had
when confronting Herod the king about his immoral
life and abuse of office. We need boldness in this hour
if we are going to fight the good fight of faith. We need
boldness:

- To confront the most difficult and unpleasant
  situations and take a sound decision.

- To handle very difficult and demanding tasks.
- To pioneer a new work and break new grounds.
- To take risks that make for progress.
- To proclaim the Word of God in sincerity and with integrity.
- To minister to the sick and the afflicted in the name of the Lord.
- To confront demons and cast them out.
- To challenge heresies, and contend earnestly for the faith which was once delivered to the saints (Jude 3).
- To stand for the truth and dare to be different. There is a critical need for the people of God to be bold at such a time as this.

Immediately Joshua became a leader of the nation of Israel after the death of Moses, the Word of the Lord came to Him. Essentially, God was asking him to be bold and strong.

Now after the death of Moses the servant of the LORD it came to pass, that the LORD spake unto Joshua the son of Nun, Moses' minister, saying, Moses my servant is dead; now therefore arise, go over this Jordan, thou, and all this people, unto the land which I do give to them, even to the children of Israel. Every place that the sole of your foot shall tread upon, that have I given unto you, as I said unto Moses. From the wilderness and this Lebanon even unto the great river, the river Euphrates, all the land of the Hittites, and unto the great sea toward the going down of the sun, shall be your coast. There shall not any man be able to stand before thee all the days of thy life:

*as I was with Moses, so I will be with thee: I will not
fail thee, nor forsake thee. Be strong and of a good
courage: for unto this people shalt thou divide for
an inheritance the land, which I sware unto their
fathers to give them. Only be thou strong and
very courageous, that thou mayest observe to do
according to all the law, which Moses my servant
commanded thee: turn not from it to the right hand
or to the left, that thou mayest prosper whithersoever
ever thou goest. This book of the law shall not
depart out of thy mouth; but thou shalt meditate
therein day and night, that thou mayest observe to
do according to all that is written therein: for then
thou shalt make thy way prosperous, and then
thou shalt have good success. Have not I commanded
manded thee? Be strong and of a good courage; be
not afraid, neither be thou dismayed: for the LORD
thy God is with thee whithersoever thou goest.*

                                        (Joshua 1:1–9)

Over and over again the Lord gave him encouragement
and asked him to be strong and bold. This is what you
need today. The same encouragement the Lord gave to
Joshua is for you also. Be strong and of good courage.

There was a time when Joab, the commander of
David's army, had to face a very difficult battle. The
Ammonites and the Syrians came against Israel. They
were so many and *'the battle was against him before
and behind'* (II Samuel 10:9). They were outnumbered
and overwhelmed. He took his brother Abishai, divided
the army into two and made a battle plan.

*When Joab saw that the front of the battle was
against him before and behind, he chose of all*

the choice men of Israel, and put them in array
against the Syrians: and the rest of the people he
delivered into the hand of Abishai his brother,
that he might put them in array against the
children of Ammon.

(II Samuel 10:9–10)

What he said next to his brother Abishai is very
instructive.

And he said, If the Syrians be too strong for me,
then thou shalt help me: but if the children of
Ammon be too strong for thee, then I will come
and help thee. Be of good courage, and let us
play the men for our people, and for the cities
of our God: and the LORD do that which seemeth
him good.

(II Samuel 10:11–12)

That is what will win the war. The Lord gave them
the victory. That always happens when people exercise
genuine faith and boldness to win and be more than a
conqueror.

Shortly before David died, he gave instructions to
Solomon, his son, who was to build the temple of
the Lord in Jerusalem. Among other things, David
emphasised the need for courage. He told Solomon
that for him to succeed in the task ahead, he must
be bold and courageous.

And thou, Solomon my son, know thou the God
of thy father, and serve him with a perfect heart
and with a willing mind: for the LORD searcheth all
hearts, and understandeth all the imaginations of
the thoughts: if thou seek him, he will be found of

*thee; but if thou forsake him, he will cast thee off
for ever. Take heed now; for the LORD hath chosen
thee to build an house for the sanctuary: be strong,
and do it.*

(I Chronicles 28:9–10)

What has the Lord chosen for you to do? What has He
committed into your hand to accomplish? Be strong and
do it. That you know that God has chosen you for the
task is not sufficient. You have to be strong to do it.
You cannot afford to be otherwise.

Lack of courage always makes people fall short of
God's expectation for them. A good example is Barak.
The Lord chose him to lead the army of Israel out
against Jabin the king of Canaan, whose army was
commanded by Sisera; of course, it took faith and
boldness to think that God was in it at all. The army
of Jabin was armed to the teeth, with nine hundred
chariots of iron. He had oppressed Israel terribly for
twenty years. It was a difficult task. However, all Barak
needed to do was to trust and obey. Since the Lord was
in it, the victory was certain.

However, rather than assuming full responsibility for
the task, he exhibited a lack of courage by insisting that
Deborah come along with him. He said that if Deborah
would not go with him then he was not going to the
battle at all. He lost the honour of the victory to a
woman. You may lose honour with the Lord and with
men if you allow lack of courage in your life.

*And Barak said unto her, If thou wilt go with me,
then I will go: but if thou wilt not go with me,
then I will not go. And she said, I will surely go
with thee: notwithstanding the journey that thou
takest shall not be for thine honour; for the LORD*

shall sell Sisera into the hand of a woman. And Deborah arose, and went with Barak to Kedesh.

                                        (Judges 4:8–9)

The earthly life of our Lord Jesus Christ was an example of courage that never fails. He was ready for any situation – a tempestuous sea; a surging crowd with diverse needs; the wild demoniac of Gadara; a lack of food to feed the hungry crowd; the loneliness resulting from the desertion by his close disciples; or the hostility of those He came to save. He was very bold and very courageous. And He has left us an example that we should follow.

Paul was one disciple of the Lord Jesus who exhibited an uncommon degree of courage. He had been so gripped with a vision of the lost that he was ready to do all he could to save them, no matter the cost. He thus threw his whole life into the task with unfailing courage. The conditions under which he worked were decidedly unfavourable. Hostilities abounded. Finances were never sufficient. Trustworthy co-labourers were so few. Yet by dint of sheer courage, he went into the battle. His courage and determination were recorded in the book of the Acts of the Apostles for us.

But none of these things move me, neither count I my life dear unto myself, so that I might finish my course with joy, and the ministry, which I have received of the Lord Jesus, to testify the gospel of the grace of God.

                                        (Acts 20:24)

Did he ever win? Of course he did! Winners never quit. Quitters never win. He got his breakthrough, and God has eternally honoured him.

You will find yourself in Paul's situations many
times. You will face unfavourable conditions and seemingly insurmountable obstacles. Let courage rise in
your heart. With faith and boldness pursue the vision
of God for your life and fight the good fight of faith.

How Can We Be Bold?

Courage does not imply activities without end. As a
man of God rightly said, 'The strong are not always
active; the wise are not always ready.' We need to
know, therefore, how we can acquire this vital weapon
of courage and boldness.

The bedrock of true courage is righteousness. When
you have a right standing and a right relationship with
God, it provides a platform for divine boldness to spring
forth. Sin and unholy living breed guilt. Guilt breeds
fear and insecurity. And fear corrodes boldness. If you
would be truly bold, your life has to be truly clean,
washed by the blood of Jesus Christ, the Lamb of
God. *'The wicked flee when no man pursueth; But the
righteous are bold as a lion'* (Proverbs 28:1).

So long as Saul the king was walking in fellowship
with God he was a conqueror. But as soon as disobedience crept into his life he became weak, fearful and
intimidated. That was why he could not face Goliath.
By not walking in righteousness, you rob yourself of
this vital weapon of war which you need against the
'Goliaths' of life. See to it that you walk in righteousness and you will find it easy to walk in boldness.

In addition, an assurance of the presence of the Lord
is a prerequisite of boldness. When the Lord is there
everything will be all right. The divine presence gives

you an assurance that you are not just about your own business but you are doing His will.

Have you ever wondered why Moses was so bold in doing all he did? Of course, it was because the presence of the Lord was with him. It was with that consciousness that he confronted Pharaoh, and the latter could not stand. By the divine presence the Red Sea parted and the rock in the wilderness gave forth water. God was there.

When Korah and Abiram rebelled against Moses in the wilderness they provoked him to anger:

> *And Moses said, Hereby ye shall know that the LORD hath sent me to do all these works; for I have not done them of mine own mind. If these men die the common death of all men, or if they be visited after the visitation of all men; then the LORD hath not sent me. But if the LORD make a new thing, and the earth open her mouth, and swallow them up, with all that appertain unto them, and they go down quick into the pit; then ye shall understand that these men have provoked the LORD.*
>
> *And it came to pass, as he had made an end of speaking all these words, that the ground clave asunder that was under them: and the earth opened her mouth, and swallowed them up, and their houses, and all the men that appertained unto Korah, and all their goods. They, and all that appertained to them, went down alive into the pit, and the earth closed upon them: and they perished from among the congregation.*
>
> (Numbers 16:28–33)

He demanded a new thing to happen and it happened. What gave him that boldness? The abiding presence of the Lord. At a point in God's dealings with him, he insisted that he would either have God's abiding presence or he would have nothing at all. He pressed his case until God gave him His Word.

> *Now therefore, I pray thee, if I have found grace in thy sight, shew me now thy way, that I may know thee, that I may find grace in thy sight: and consider that this nation is thy people. And he said, My presence shall go with thee, and I will give thee rest.*
>
> (Exodus 33:13–14)

Your greatest asset in life is the presence of God in your life. It will make you great. It will make you a blessing. Do what Moses did. Spend much time in the presence of the Lord, and let His glory come upon your life. Let Him lead you into whatever and wherever He wants you to go. Let Him take the initiative. When He is present with you, boldness will come naturally.

Beside this, a man can also develop boldness as a result of a Word from God. When the Word of God comes to a man it inspires faith and confidence. God spoke to Joshua and he was strong. The Word of the Lord came to Jeremiah and it filled him with courage. When God speaks something happens. Beloved, take time to receive a Word from God. It will lift you from fear to faith.

How does this word of courage come? By spending time with the Bible, prayerfully meditating in the Word of God. Do not be in a hurry. Give it the time it takes. When the Word comes alive in your heart you will be bold as a lion. Moreover, when a man comes under the anointing of the Holy Spirit, he is clothed with incredible power and boldness. All through the Bible, every time people came under the power of the Holy Spirit, they began to manifest a degree of boldness that is totally out of this world. Samson was a different man while under the power of the Holy Spirit. He could run through a troop of soldiers and leap over the wall. He was not afraid of any man or group of people. The prophet Micah says, *'But truly I am full of power by the spirit of the LORD, and of judgment, and of might, to declare unto Jacob his transgression, and to Israel his sin'* (Micah 3:8).

The moment the anointing came upon David he received boldness to face and kill first a bear, then a lion, and then Goliath of Gath. Peter and the rest of the disciples were anything but bold before they received the power of the Holy Spirit. They were so fearful they had to hide behind closed doors. They were too scared to openly identify with Jesus. At the hour of His betrayal they all ran away. But then the Holy Spirit came upon them. They were baptised with the Holy Spirit and came under the anointing of God from heaven. And that made the difference. They became bold and began to preach the Gospel. Signs and wonders began to happen by their hands and the whole of Jerusalem was stirred up. The anointing brought boldness. The anointing made them strong.

Pray For Boldness

I took some time to study the prayer life of the early Church as recorded in the Acts of the Apostles. They prayed a lot. They kept a prayer watch. They continued steadfastly in prayer. They gave themselves to prayer and the ministry of the Word. Among the key issues they prayed for was boldness.

And now, Lord, behold their threatenings: and grant unto thy servants, that with all boldness they may speak thy word, by stretching forth thine hand to heal; and that signs and wonders may be done by the name of thy holy child Jesus.

And when they had prayed, the place was shaken where they were assembled together; and they were all filled with the Holy Ghost, and they spake the word of God with boldness.

(Acts 4:29–31)

Boldness to preach the Word! What a prayer! And they were answered exactly.

And with great power gave the apostles witness of the resurrection of the Lord Jesus: and great grace was upon them all.

(Acts 4:33)

We need boldness to perform signs, wonders and miracles in the name of Jesus. We need boldness to confront our generation with the claims of Christ. We need boldness to plant and establish the Church of the Lord Jesus Christ. Boldness is a vital weapon of victory in spiritual warfare. Therefore, pray for boldness.

Chapter Thirteen

Wisdom Is The Principal Thing

Wisdom is the principal thing; therefore get wisdom: And with all thy getting get understanding.
                                                            (Proverbs 4:7)

Wisdom is one of the principal weapons needed for effective spiritual warfare. A man may have all other things going for him but if he does not walk in wisdom he will be a miserable failure. While wisdom has promoted and exalted so many people, lack of it has been the downfall of not a few. It is important to acquire the weapon of wisdom for victory in the battle of life.

I was present at a conference in 1986 where Reinhardt Bonkke was sharing the vision the Lord had given him of a 'blood-washed Africa' i.e. Africa washed with the blood of Jesus. The burden became heavy, for him to move in to begin to gather the over-ripe, harvest field of Africa. But the task looked impossible. He prayed more intensely, asking the Lord how it would be done. He said there was one word the Holy Spirit kept bringing into his mind on how to get the work done. That word was strategy! He asked for wisdom and the Lord led him to devise a plan that eventually opened to him the doors to most African nations. Divine wisdom has played a crucial role in his successful operations in Africa.

The place of wisdom in the end-time battle cannot be over-emphasised.

Anytime God wants to use a man for an outstanding work in the Kingdom, He anoints such a man with the Spirit of wisdom. When that man then moves into the task he succeeds. Not just because he possesses superior knowledge, or because he has more money or greater strength. He succeeds by the application of divine wisdom.

There is no task so difficult that it cannot be done. There are no difficulties big enough to successfully stand in the way. There may be uncountable adversaries, there may be much opposition, criticism and prejudice. The basic tools needed may not be initially available. But success and a breakthrough comes when divine wisdom is put to work.

Let me share with you a few examples of people in the Scriptures who had very difficult tasks to perform, but were specifically anointed by God with the Spirit of wisdom. Remember, God has no favourites. All those who love Him with all their hearts and are prepared to do His will are His favourites. If you too will ask Him for wisdom He will give it to you abundantly.

When the tabernacle was to be constructed in the wilderness, the Lord called Bezaleel the son of Uri by name and asked him to do it, under Moses' instructions.

And the Lord spake unto Moses, saying, See, I have called by name Bezaleel the son of Uri, the son of Hur, of the tribe of Judah: and I have filled him with the spirit of God, in wisdom, and in understanding, and in knowledge, and in all manner of workmanship, to devise cunning works, to work in gold, and in silver, and in brass, and in cutting of stones, to set them, and in carving of timber, to work in all manner of workmanship.

(Exodus 31:1–5)

Remember that the Holy Spirit is the Spirit of wisdom and understanding and knowledge (Isaiah 11:2). Bezaleel was specifically anointed for wisdom to do the work of the tabernacle and indeed, he finished the job. Wisdom never makes a failure out of a man. Wisdom makes you finish your work and deliver the goods.

Shortly before the death of Moses, the Lord told him to lay his hands upon Joshua and anoint him to lead the people of Israel. So the Spirit of wisdom came upon Joshua for effective leadership.

And Joshua the son of Nun was full of the spirit of wisdom; for Moses had laid his hands upon him: and the children of Israel hearkened unto him, and did as the Lord commanded Moses.

(Deuteronomy 34:9)

Because the Spirit of wisdom rested upon Joshua, the people of Israel obeyed him. There is the need for wisdom in leadership. This comes by the Holy Spirit.

We are all familiar with the story of Solomon and his remarkable wisdom. It came to him as a gift from God shortly after he became the king of Israel. Because he walked in wisdom he excelled in all leadership virtues and dealt wisely in all affairs of his kingdom. What about our Lord Jesus Christ? Hundreds of years before He was born, prophecies about Him were clear that He would be anointed with the Spirit of wisdom.

And there shall come forth a rod out of the stem of Jesse, and a Branch shall grow out of his roots:

*and the spirit of the LORD shall rest upon him, the
spirit of wisdom and understanding, the spirit of
counsel and might, the spirit of knowledge and of
the fear of the LORD.*

(Isaiah 11:1–2)

There it is. He was anointed with the Spirit of wisdom
and understanding. When he came into the world He
literally fulfilled that prophecy. The Bible records that
'*[He] grew, and waxed strong in spirit, filled with
wisdom: and the grace of God was upon him*' (Luke
2:40). Even though He is God, yet as a man He had
this all-important weapon of wisdom and used it effectively to defeat the adversaries and finish His work on
earth.

As His disciples, we are to follow in His steps to
advance the Kingdom of God. Paul walked in wisdom,
therefore he succeeded.

It was also written about Stephen that the adversary
of the Gospel could not withstand or resist the wisdom
and the Spirit with which he spoke (Acts 6:10). This
is how effective spiritual warfare is to be fought these
last days by the application of wisdom.

I know some ministers of the Gospel who are truly
called of God, filled with the Holy Spirit, very prayerful,
but are not successful. They go from one frustration into
another, from debt further into debt, from crisis into
crisis, simply because they do not walk in wisdom. I
know a man who has been in the ministry for over
twenty years and is a miserable failure. He lives a
holy life. He studies the Scriptures and prays a lot.
He puts in so much labour and effort but there is no
visible progress. No plan. No strategy for development.
No office set-up. He is never organised. He just moves
from one activity into another as the demands come.

This is not wisdom. God wants you to succeed in every aspect of your life. Therefore He wants you to be organised. One of the keys to success is wisdom.

The Wisdom Of God

Our God is the God of wisdom. He is *'the only wise God'* (I Timothy 1:17). All that He does is done in wisdom.

> *O LORD, how manifold are thy works!*
> *In wisdom hast thou made them all:*
> *The earth is full of thy riches.*
>
> (Psalm 104:24)

As I was meditating on this scripture sometime ago, it struck me forcibly that wisdom is crucial to success in life. Indeed the works of God are manifold, yet there is no confusion or conflict. This is because He does everything wisely. It is His wisdom that has given birth to the riches of the earth.

> *The LORD by wisdom hath founded the earth;*
> *By understanding hath he established the*
>   *heavens.*
> *By his knowledge the depths are broken up,*
> *And the clouds drop down the dew.*
>
> (Proverbs 3:19–20)

All that God does, He does with wisdom. He expects us to do the same. The Bible explains that there are two kinds of wisdom. There is the wisdom that comes from above and there is the wisdom that comes from below. The latter is what the people of this world employ in their dealings. It is selfish and gives birth to all strife, wars, envy, confusion, and every evil work.

'*This wisdom descendeth not from above, but is earthly, sensual, devilish*' (James 3:15). This is the wisdom of the devil. It is behind all the tricks, magics, deceptions, corruption, perversion, oppression and other evils we have in the world today. This is not the kind of wisdom being advocated in this book.

The kind of wisdom you are to covet and seek after is the wisdom that comes from God.

> *But the wisdom that is from above is first pure, then peaceable, gentle, and easy to be intreated, full of mercy and good fruits, without partiality, and without hypocrisy.*
>
> (James 3:17)

This wisdom is divine. It is different from cunning craftiness. It is not self-centred. It seeks to glorify the Lord. It is pure. It never indulges in, or encourages, anything immoral, ungodly or shady. It is peaceable; it does not involve oppression, extortion, strife or bloodshed. It is gentle; not rude nor crude; not violent nor volatile. It is submissive. It easily forgives and it accommodates others' shortcomings and deficiencies. It is neither judgmental nor castigating. It is full of mercy and compassion and it is without partiality or hypocrisy. In other words, this wisdom is an embodiment of integrity. This is the kind of wisdom that is a principal weapon of spiritual warfare. A man in possession of this wisdom cannot be moved. He will always be ahead of the adversary.

There are people who go into all manner of shady and questionable behaviours, and they call it wisdom. They manipulate and lie to get money. Others give false reports or astronomical exaggerations of the truth in order to gain respect. Anything that does not flow out of purity, integrity and sincerity cannot be said to be pure wisdom. Such eventually destroys people that engage in them. But the righteous shall never be shaken.

> A good man showeth favour, and lendeth:
> He will guide his affairs with discretion.
> Surely he shall not be moved for ever:
> The righteous shall be in everlasting
>   remembrance.
> He shall not be afraid of evil tidings:
> His heart is fixed, trusting in the LORD.
> His heart is established, he shall not be afraid,
> Until he see his desire upon his enemies.
>
> (Psalm 112:5–8)

The Crucial Place Of Wisdom

The Bible is very clear on the crucial place of wisdom in the life of a man. As a matter of fact, wisdom is referred to as the principal thing. The Bible says that with all you ever acquire in life you must have wisdom. 'Wisdom is the principal thing; therefore get wisdom: And with all thy getting get understanding' (Proverbs 4:7).

The whole book of Proverbs majors on the subject of wisdom and how to acquire it. At the onset, the goal of the book is stated to be to 'know wisdom and instruction; To perceive the words of understanding; To receive the instruction of wisdom, Justice, and *judgment, and equity'* (Proverbs 1:2–3). If a subject is that important for God to specifically devote a whole book of the Bible to it then it ought to be important to you. It means, then, that a man neglects wisdom only to his own peril. Blessed, however, is the man that finds wisdom. (See Proverbs 3:13–26.)

Wisdom is held out to be more precious than rubies. The Bible says that *'all the things thou desire are not to be compared unto wisdom'*. Here is a list of some of the blessings that come your way by walking in wisdom.

- Long life – you enjoy long life by walking in wisdom (Proverbs 3:16).
- Riches and wealth – a man walking in wisdom will be wealthy (v16).
- Honour – there is honour for the man who walks in wisdom (v16).
- Peace – there is peace through wisdom (v17).
- Happiness and joy – wisdom will give birth to these (v18).
- Creativity – you are creative and productive through wisdom (v19).
- Life – wisdom is life to your soul. Many have died through foolishness (v18).
- Grace – wisdom makes a man graceful (v22).
- Safety and security – as you walk in wisdom, nothing makes you afraid. You are secure (v23).
- Protection – this also comes by walking in wisdom (v23).
- Confidence – wisdom makes a man confident. Shame is the reward of foolishness (v24).

You can see here that wisdom will simply put you on top in life and will make your face to shine. Many people make the pursuit of wealth their supreme pursuit in life. To others it is political power; to others it is fame. But when you are in possession of divine wisdom, you have something that is more precious than all of these put together.

For wisdom is a defence, and money is a defence: but the excellency of knowledge is, that wisdom giveth life to them that have it.

(Ecclesiastes 7:12)

Wisdom strengtheneth the wise more than ten mighty men which are in the city.

(Ecclesiastes 7:19)

All these have I proved by wisdom: I said, I will be wise; but it was far from me.

(Ecclesiastes 7:23)

How Does Wisdom Come?

It must be emphasised here that this wisdom that is from above comes from God. There are various means of acquiring this wisdom but it must be understood that God is the only source of it.

For the LORD giveth wisdom:
Out of his mouth cometh knowledge and
    understanding.
He layeth up sound wisdom for the righteous:
He is a buckler to them that walk uprightly.

(Proverbs 2:6–7)

By the Word
The first way by which God imparts this wisdom is through the Word. Do you really want to be filled with

wisdom from above? Then you have to take the Word
of God seriously and spend quality time with it on a
daily basis, and the wisdom of God shall be imparted
to you.

Speaking about the effect the Word of God has on
man, David said:

> The law of the LORD is perfect, converting the
>   soul:
> The testimony of the LORD is sure, making wise
>   the simple.
>
> (Psalm 19:7)

Do you really want to be made wise? Then pay close
attention to the Word. The Word of God will give
you wisdom that is above whatever can be acquired
by experience of life or any process of learning. You
receive God's own wisdom as you meditate in the Word
of God.

> I have more understanding than all my teachers:
> For thy testimonies are my meditation.
> I understand more than the ancients,
> Because I keep thy precepts.
>
> (Psalm 119:99–100)

This is more than knowing the Word or being able to
quote or teach it to others. This involves knowing and
practising the Word of God. It is the doing of the Word
of God that leads into practical wisdom for life. It is
as you obey the Scriptures that you walk in wisdom.
This was exactly what the Lord told Joshua after he
became the leader of Israel. God made it clear that

for him to deal wisely in the affairs of life he had to take the Word of God seriously and diligently apply it in his life.

> *This book of the law shall not depart out of thy mouth; but thou shalt meditate therein day and night, that thou mayest observe to do according to all that is written therein: for then thou shalt make thy way prosperous, and then thou shalt have good success.*
>
> (Joshua 1:8)

God told Joshua to do three things:

- The Word must not depart from his mouth.
- He should meditate in it day and night.
- He should obey all that is written in the Word.

God told Joshua that if he did the above, He would see to it that he walked in prosperity and dealt wisely in the affairs of life.

Beloved, the wisdom of God will permeate every area of your life if you truly dedicate yourself to walking in the Word of God. It is the Word that will guide your feet into the way of wisdom.

You can also acquire wisdom through wise counsel. God is the only one that is all-wise. We human beings, no matter how holy, godly or prayerful, no matter how much of the Word of God we know, because of our limited knowledge and ability we still need the godly counsel of others. *'Where no counsel is, the people fall: But in the multitude of counsellors there is safety'* (Proverbs 11:14). In addition, the Bible makes it clear that it is by wise counsel that effective warfare can be waged. Before a nation sends her army to war, a war council meeting is held first. All the generals meet and discuss and lay out their strategies. Until this is done they cannot go to war. If this is the case in the physical, how much more in spiritual warfare. Mature and godly counsel is needed in order to be victorious in spiritual warfare. *'For by wise counsel thou shalt make thy war: and in multitude of counsellors there is safety'* (Proverbs 24:6).

As crucial as counsels are, however, we must understand that counsel that contradicts the Word of God in any form is the counsel of the ungodly. It could be given by your husband, wife, parents, close associates or any other person. Nevertheless, so long as it does not agree with the Word of God it must be rejected.

> *Blessed is the man that walketh not in the*
> *   counsel of the ungodly,*
> *Nor standeth in the way of sinners,*
> *Nor sitteth in the seat of the scornful.*
> *But his delight is in the law of the LORD;*
> *And in his law doth he meditate day and night.*
> *And he shall be like a tree planted by the rivers*
> *   of water,*
> *That bringeth forth his fruit in his season;*
> *His leaf also shall not wither;*
> *And whatsoever he doeth shall prosper.*
>
> (Psalm 1:1–3)

Also, any counsel you receive must agree with what the Holy Spirit is clearly telling you to do. You are not to be led only by human counselling. It should confirm what the Holy Spirit has already told you clearly.

So many people, after having heard clearly from God, go to seek the advice of men. Often their purpose is not to get a confirmation of God's perfect will but to find an excuse to escape from their responsibility to obey the voice of the Holy Spirit. This is what Paul refused to do. As soon as it was clear to him that God was calling him into the ministry, he did not run around seeking to dodge the call. He refused to allow the flesh to get in the way of God. He stepped out in obedience and God honoured his faith.

But when it pleased God, who separated me from my mother's womb, and called me by his grace, to reveal his Son in me, that I might preach him among the heathen; immediately I conferred not with flesh and blood: neither went I up to Jerusalem to them which were apostles before me; but I went into Arabia, and returned again unto Damascus.

(Galatians 1:15–17)

You are to seek and take advice when you really are not sure of God's perfect will and are eager to know and to do it. After discovering the will of God and the directions He would want you to take in life, do not go for counselling any more on that, otherwise you will be confused and confounded.

Above all, no matter what advice men give you, God's counsel is expressed in His Word and in the leading of the Holy Spirit, which must be supreme. It should not be compromised. If you are willing and obedient, you will be blessed beyond all imagination. *'If you be willing and obedient, ye shall eat the good of the land'* (Isaiah 1:19). *'If they obey and serve him, they shall spend*

their days in prosperity, and their years in pleasures'
(Job 36:11).

By the anointing

Thirdly, wisdom comes through the anointing of the
Holy Spirit. He is the Spirit of wisdom. This has
been explained earlier on in this chapter. I have seen
many people's lives changed as they come under the
anointing of the Holy Spirit. God will see to it that you
are anointed with wisdom to accomplish the particular
task He has given to you. Therefore, ask God to anoint
you and He will.

> *If ye then, being evil, know how to give good gifts
> unto your children: how much more shall your
> heavenly Father give the Holy Spirit to them that
> ask him?*
>
> (Luke 11:13)

By association

Fourth, to be wise, you have to walk with the wise. It
is important who you associate with. You are to love
everybody but you should choose your friends. The
people who surround you and the people that you
relate with go a long way in moulding your opinion
and in influencing your decisions. If they are fools
then you are in for trouble. It is important to walk
with the wise. *'He that walketh with wise men shall
be wise: but a companion of fools shall be destroyed'*
(Proverbs 13:20).

Of course this is not advocating a selfish motivation
in your choice of friends, such as running after people
because of what you think you might benefit from them.
Rather, this is a call for real relationship, fellowship
and sharing that are mutually beneficial. God will use

certain individuals to build you up and you will also make a solid contribution to their lives. They must be people who are capable of impacting your life positively. You are not to stand alone while fighting spiritual warfare. There should be friends who will assist you along the way. These should, however, be wise, Spirit-filled people who are dedicated to following the Lord with all of their hearts.

Iron sharpeneth iron;
So a man sharpeneth the countenance of his
*   friend.*

(Proverbs 27:17)

The wise shall inherit glory;
But shame shall be the promotion of fools.

(Proverbs 3:35)

In the early Church, when men were needed to serve at the tables as deacons, one of the qualifications required of them was that they must be full of wisdom. This requirement was as basic as being filled with the Holy Spirit. It is vital that Christians are not just full of the Holy Spirit but also full of wisdom. *'But we will give ourselves continually to prayer, and to the ministry of the word'* (Acts 6:4).

It is with such people that are full of the Holy Spirit and wisdom that you should associate. You will find this beneficial both to you and to God's Kingdom if you have a teachable spirit. Because, in order to be wise you must be teachable. Learn to keep quiet and listen. Silence often is golden. Learn to listen to others and learn. You should not be a know all. Such people are full of pride. They claim they know everything and are not ready to admit their need. They do not ask questions. They are

opinionated and are always right. The Bible calls such
people fools. But a wise man will use every opportunity
available to him to learn. He will learn from the wise,
from the fool, from the young, from the old. He will learn
from everything in order to increase his own wisdom
and be more informed.

It is the quest for wisdom that drives a man to
buy books, tapes, journals, and anything else that
will positively contribute to his growth. Be wise. Be
a learner. Let God use anyone and anything He can to
instruct you. '*A wise man will hear, and will increase
learning; And a man of understanding shall attain unto
wise counsels*' (Proverbs 1:5).

By prayer

Lastly, you are to pray and ask the Lord to fill you with
wisdom from above. Wisdom to succeed as a husband
or wife. Wisdom, as a student, to excel in your studies;
wisdom to pastor your church effectively and reach
your goal. Wisdom to discover your ministry and fulfil
it. Wisdom to succeed in your career and business.
Wisdom to prosper in every aspect of your life.

Before Solomon could manifest his extraordinary
wisdom, he asked for it from God and the Lord gave it
to him. God had told him to ask for whatever he wanted
and it would be done for him. He could have asked for
money, or long life, or victory over his enemies. But
he asked for wisdom. And God gave it to him. It was
this wisdom that eventually gave birth to all the other
things that he needed or desired. Wisdom will do the
same to whoever asks for it.

*In Gibeon the LORD appeared to Solomon in a
dream by night: and God said, Ask what I shall*

give thee. And Solomon said, Thou hast shewed unto thy servant David my father great mercy, according as he walked before thee in truth, and in righteousness, and in uprightness of heart with thee; and thou hast kept for him this great kindness, that thou hast given him a son to sit on his throne, as it is this day. And now, O LORD my God, thou hast made thy servant king instead of David my father: and I am but a little child: I know not how to go out or come in. And thy servant is in the midst of thy people which thou hast chosen, a great people, that cannot be numbered nor counted for multitude. Give therefore thy servant an understanding heart to judge thy people, that I may discern between good and bad: for who is able to judge this thy so great a people?

And the speech pleased the LORD, that Solomon had asked this thing. And God said unto him, Because thou hast asked this thing, and hast not asked for thyself long life; neither hast asked riches for thyself, nor hast asked the life of thine enemies; but hast asked for thyself understanding to discern judgment; behold, I have done according to thy words: lo, I have given thee a wise and an understanding heart; so that there was none like thee before thee, neither after thee shall any arise like unto thee. And I have also given thee that which thou hast not asked, both riches, and honour: so that there shall not be any among the kings like unto thee all thy days. And if thou wilt walk in my ways, to keep my statutes and my commandments, as thy father David did walk, then I will lengthen thy days.

(I Kings 3:5–14)

And God gave Solomon wisdom and understand-
ing exceeding much, and largeness of heart, even
as the sand that is on the sea shore. And Solomon's
wisdom excelled the wisdom of all the children
of the east country, and all the wisdom of Egypt.
For he was wiser than all men; than Ethan the
Ezrahite, and Heman, and Chalcol, and Darda,
the sons of Mahol: and his fame was in all nations
round about.

(I Kings 4:29–31)

And the LORD gave Solomon wisdom, as he prom-
ised him . . .

(I Kings 5:12a)

It should be noted how Solomon took time to really
pray, asking for wisdom. He was not arrogant. He saw
himself as a 'little child' who did not know 'how to
go out or come in'. He also realised the enormity of
the task the Lord had given him to do and the critical
need for wisdom. He then prayed with passion, asking
for a baptism of wisdom from on high. And the Lord
answered his prayer. He still answers the cry of those
who would ask Him for wisdom today and He is able to
do exceedingly abundantly above all that we can ask or
think, according to the power that works in us.

God has given a definite promise in His Word that
if you will ask for wisdom, He will give it to you.
Therefore, ask today and you shall receive from God.

If any of you lack wisdom, let him ask of God, that
giveth to all men liberally, and upbraideth not;
and it shall be given him. But let him ask in faith,
nothing wavering. For he that wavereth is like a
wave of the sea driven with the wind and tossed.

(James 1:5–6)

As we close this chapter, I must bring to your attention a crucial issue the Lord raised with Solomon when He bestowed divine wisdom upon him. Wisdom which if you ask Him for it today He will give you. However, you should note what the Lord told Solomon.

> *And if thou wilt walk in my ways, to keep my statutes and my commandments, as thy father David did walk, then I will lengthen thy days.*
>
> (I Kings 3:14)

Take note of the 'if', then you will walk in wisdom for a very long time to come. This is important. Therefore, beloved, make up your mind not only to ask and receive wisdom today, but to walk in wisdom all the days of your life, living in the fear of the Lord and in obedience to His Word.

Thus you will find yourself at the beginning of wisdom everyday, not at the end of it. Walking in the fear of God is your guarantee of endless wisdom from on high.

> *The fear of the LORD is the beginning of wisdom: And the knowledge of the holy is understanding.*
>
> (Proverbs 9:10)

Chapter Fourteen

The Just Shall Live By Faith

There is a statement that occurs four times in the Bible, once in the Old Testament and three times in the New. When God repeats a statement, over and over again, the issue involved must be crucial. We should pay close attention to it. The Bible says:

But the just shall live by his faith.

Habakkuk 2:4b

The just shall live by faith.

Romans 1:17

For, The just shall live by faith.

Galatians 3:11

Now the just shall live by faith.

Hebrews 10:38

As believers in Christ Jesus, we are to live by faith. Faith is a crucial weapon in spiritual warfare. There can be neither success nor victory without faith. It is by faith we live. It is by faith we receive any gift, any blessing, any favour from God. The Christian faith is supernatural from A to Z and it is faith that links us with the supernatural. That is why Christianity is called 'the faith'. The Bible declares that without faith it is impossible to please God. Faith is absolutely essential if you will relate to Him and if you will win in the battle of life in which we are engaged.

But without faith it is impossible to please him: for he that cometh to God must believe that he is, and that he is a rewarder of them that diligently seek him.

(Hebrews 11:6)

What Is Faith?

Faith has been variously described by Bible scholars and theologians. Faith is to believe and act on the Word of God. When you believe what God says in His Word and you step out to act on it, that is faith. God said it; I believe it; that settles it – that is the language of faith. *'Now faith is the substance of things hoped for, the evidence of things not seen'* (Hebrews 11:1).

Paraphrasing the biblical definition of faith above, the Living Bible puts it this way:

What is faith? It is the confident assurance that something we want is going to happen. It is the certainty that what we hope for is waiting for us, even though we cannot see it up ahead.

(Hebrews 11:1 LB)

The basis of faith is God's Word. That God has said it in His Word makes it certain. When you are confident and sure that what you want is going to happen, according to the Word of God, that is faith. When you are certain and convinced that what you desire, on the basis of God's Word, shall come; that is faith. Faith sees beyond the present prevailing circumstances into the fulfilment of God's Word. Faith refuses to look at what is seen which is temporal, but sees that which is not seen, which is eternal. Faith takes its stand on the Word of God and boldly declares that it shall be done, no matter what is taking place now.

That was the attitude of Abraham. After receiving God's Word that he and Sarah would have a child, he believed it. Even though years elapsed without the promise becoming a reality and the enemy kept attacking him severely with doubts, he still held on to God's Word. He knew he was dealing with a God that cannot lie. He knew all else might fail but the Word of the Lord cannot fall to the ground. He was fully persuaded that what God had promised He was able to perform. He waited. And through faith and patience, He obtained the fulfilment of the promise of God.

(As it is written, I have made thee a father of many nations,) before him whom he believed, even God, who quickeneth the dead, and calleth those things which be not as though they were. Who against hope believed in hope, that he might become the father of many nations; according to that which was spoken, So shall thy seed be. And being not weak in faith, he considered not his own body now dead, when he was about an hundred years old, neither yet the deadness of Sarah's womb: he staggered not at the promise of God through unbelief; but was strong in faith, giving glory to God; and being fully persuaded that, what he had promised, he was able also to perform.

(Romans 4:17–21)

You need to live by faith at all times, in order to over-come the devices of the devil on issues as fundamental as your belief in God, or the veracity of His Word.

I remember a time when the enemy attacked my mind over the claims of the Lord Jesus Christ as God and Saviour of mankind. I was severely troubled. I had just finished a study of the books of Samuel in the Bible and I came out of that study with a solid conviction that Jehovah the God of Israel is the true and living God. What I discovered about God in those two books of the Scriptures greatly strengthened my conviction about the omnipotence of God. Then the questions came, How can this be the same God of the New Testament? How could Jesus possibly be co-equal and co-eternal with this awesome God? For days, I battled with questions upon questions. I prayed, I searched the Scriptures eagerly, but the more questions I resolved, the more arose in my mind. One morning after a time of prayer, the Holy Spirit brought these two scriptures to me, and I used them in prayer to demolish the arguments of the devil.

But in those sacrifices there is a remembrance again made of sins every year.

(Hebrews 10:3)

Above all, taking the shield of faith, wherewith ye shall be able to quench all the fiery darts of the wicked.

(Ephesians 6:16)

That morning, the Lord gave me clear answers to the questions bothering my heart. I soon discovered that it was not argument, but faith, that would win the battle. Simply believing the Word of God put my heart to rest. I do not need to see before I believe. I believe, therefore

I shall see the glory of God. For close to two decades now since that crisis, I have boldly proclaimed Jesus Christ as Lord and Saviour from the Scriptures to countless multitudes. God has been pleased to confirm that truth with signs and wonders and healings according to His Word. Indeed, *'the just shall live by faith'*.

The enemy may also attack with sickness or disease while at the same time contending that the Word of God concerning divine healing is not true. What do you do? Do you walk by what you see and cast aside the Word of God? That is the exact time you should prove that you believe God's Word, that you are healed by the stripes of the Lord Jesus. Whether the symptoms linger or not, hold on to the Word of God. Let God be true and every man a liar.

Sometimes, you may come face to face with a crisis or a danger, as did Shadrach, Meshach and Abednego. They were ordered to either bow down to Nebuchadnezzar's golden image or be thrown into the fiery furnace. If they had been moved by the dominating personality of the king, or the golden image he had set up or the burning fiery furnace, they would have faltered and fallen. But they stood by faith. They refused to be intimidated. They did not focus their attention on what was happening around them. They focused on the Lord and His promises. The Bible says *'Thou wilt keep him in perfect peace, whose mind is stayed on thee: because he trusteth in thee'* (Isaiah 26:3). They were at peace and handled the situation heroically, because they chose to walk by faith. There is no crisis that may come, where you will not be in complete control, when you walk by faith.

Therefore, beloved, in every situation, determine to walk by faith. At any given time you will be open to two voices. The voice of faith and the voice of fear. Faith will affirm the Word of God, telling you to step out on it, irrespective of what is happening; fear will tell you that believing God's Word is unrealistic and you will be fooling yourself if you do. Choose to walk by faith. Reject the voice of fear. You will always find yourself on top.

Faith Always Gets Results

Here is where faith is different from presumption. Faith cannot fail. It always obtains results. This is because it stands on the unfailing Word of God. The Bible has this to say about the heroes of faith who went ahead of us. *'For by it [faith] the elders obtained a good report'* (Hebrews 11:2).

By faith the elders got results. Whatever you want to receive must be by faith. Whether it is a good report or healing, prosperity or deliverance or a new anointing. If you must obtain it from God then it is by faith.

When genuine faith is at work, based on the Word of God, as inspired to you by the Holy Spirit, there will be a definite result. Consider again the case of Shadrach, Meshach and Abednego. They spoke in faith to the king that their God was going to deliver them.

Shadrach, Meshach, and Abednego, answered and said to the king, O Nebuchadnezzar, we are not careful to answer thee in this matter. If it be so, our God who we serve is able to deliver us from the burning fiery furnace, and he will deliver us out of thine hand, O king. But if not, be it known unto thee, O king, that we will not serve thy gods, nor worship the golden image which thou hast set up.

(Daniel 3:16–18)

The king was very angry. He ordered the furnace to be heated seven times over and he threw them into it at once. Were they consumed? No. The fire only succeeded in breaking their chains so they could walk up and down in the midst of the fire. Because faith honours God, God also honours faith.

What about Abraham? He chose to wait for the fulfilment of God's Word even though all physical evidence seemed contrary. He was already an old man, and Sarah his wife was too old to have a child.

Yet, because God had spoken to him personally, he believed and refused to doubt. Did he obtain the promise? Certainly! No doubt. At God's appointed time Isaac was born. We also are to be followers of those who through faith and patience inherited the promises.

> *And we desire that every one of you do shew the same diligence to the full assurance of hope unto the end: that ye be not slothful, but followers of them who through faith and patience inherit the promises.*
>
> *For when God made promise to Abraham, because he could swear by no greater, he sware by himself, saying, Surely blessing I will bless thee, and multiplying I will multiply thee. And so, after he had patiently endured, he obtained the promise.*
>
> (Hebrews 6:11–15)

Faith Is Your Shield

As you press on in spiritual warfare, the enemy will direct his fiery darts against you with bitter hatred and ferocious opposition. He will attack your home, your health, your finances, your integrity and your testimonies. There shall be cunningly devised temptations, oppositions and terrible persecutions. People will talk about you and unjustly criticise you. Your friendships and relationships will be tried. But faith is your shield. By it you can ward off and quench all the fiery darts of the enemy. By it you can overcome every opposition and win every battle. Take your shield of faith, beloved, for faith is the victory that overcomes the world. If you live by faith you will live on top.

> *For whatsoever is born of God overcometh the world: and this is the victory that overcometh the world, even our faith.*
>
> (I John 5:4)

Kinds of Faith

There are different kinds of faith.

There are people with no faith. These are people who face situations from a position of unbelief. Rather than seeing God and believing His Word, they see the devil, and the problems. They fear and fret. They complain and moan. To such comes our Lord's reprimand, '... *How is it that ye have no faith?*' or put in another form, '*Where is your faith?*' (Mark 4:40).

There are people who operate only at the level of historical faith. They believe in the truthfulness and accuracy of the Scriptures and in all the key doctrines of the Christian faith. However, it remains a dry belief in their heads, it has not got down into their hearts. It has not changed or saved them. They are not born again. To such people the proposition of James is very appropriate.

Thou believest that there is one God; thou doest well: the devils also believe, and tremble.

Ye see then how that by works a man is justified, and not by faith only.

(James 2:19,24)

We need to go beyond the level of head-knowledge faith and truly believe Jesus as our Saviour and Lord and be saved.

There is therefore, a saving faith. At this level of faith, a man believes with his heart in the Lord Jesus as His personal Saviour and Lord and he is justified. He confesses with his mouth that Jesus is his Lord and he is saved. It is saving faith that makes a man experience the salvation of God by grace. It is this faith we must have, otherwise we cannot enter into the Kingdom of heaven. The Bible makes this very clear.

That if thou shalt confess with thy mouth the Lord Jesus, and shalt believe in thine heart that God hath raised him from the dead, thou shalt be saved. For with the heart man believeth unto righteousness; and with the mouth confession is made unto salvation.

(Romans 10:9–10)

For those with faith, there is a need for confession with the mouth and believing with the heart. This is because it is with the heart that man believes unto righteousness and it is with the mouth confession is made unto salvation. You are not only to believe with your heart, you must also confess with your mouth that Jesus Christ is your Lord.

For by grace are ye saved through faith; and that not of yourselves: it is the gift of God: not of works, lest any man should boast. For we are his workmanship, created in Christ Jesus unto good works, which God hath before ordained that we should walk in them.

(Ephesians 2:8–10)

Moreover, there is a faith for living. After receiving Jesus Christ as your Saviour, you are to continue in the faith appropriating the promises of God in His Word, in your daily walk with Him and to meet your daily needs. You need to receive the power of the Holy Spirit, enjoy divine healing and health, flow in God's prosperity and bring into practical reality every part of the Word of God in your life. All this is through faith – different from the saving faith. There are many people who are saved and are genuinely born again, but because they do not build their faith and move beyond the saving faith, they are never able to appropriate God's promises in His Word. Hence, they remain sick, oppressed, tormented, poor and frustrated. If they die they will go to heaven. However because they do not live by faith here on earth, they never enjoy the fullness of God's blessings and the abundant life that Jesus Christ has purchased for us.

That is why the Bible says *'the just shall live by faith'*. As you live by faith, you will take every aspect of the Word of God and personally appropriate it for your blessing and edification, sanctification and victory.

Yet there is also faith for the miraculous. This is a definite gift of the Holy Spirit. All believers do not have this faith for it is given to people as the Spirit of God wills. It is with this faith we raise the dead, cast out demons, perform miracles and turn hopeless situations around. It was through the instrumentality of this gift

that Moses parted the Red Sea for the redeemed of the
Lord to pass through. It was by this gift that Joshua
stopped the sun for a whole day. It was by this gift of
faith that all those heroes of faith achieved great things
for God and His Kingdom. Faith for the miraculous is
a definite gift of the Holy Spirit for all who believe and
ask for it.

However, there is another faith that goes beyond the
veil of the physical to lay a hold on spiritual realities.
This is a faith that does not look at the things that are
seen but the things that are not seen. You know that
the things that are seen are temporal, while the things
that are not seen are eternal.

We speak about God.

While we look not at the things which are seen,
but at the things which are not seen: for the things
which are seen are temporal; but the things which
are not seen are eternal.

(II Corinthians 4:18)

How do we know He exists? It is by faith. We speak
about heaven, the glorious mansions that Jesus has
gone to prepare for us, the pearly gates and the singing
angels. How do we know these are true? It is by faith.
This faith goes beyond the material things of this world
like cars, houses, finances, husbands, wives, children,
clothes, a job, and all the good things of life. It sees
eternal realities in the light of the glory of God.

It was this kind of faith that made Abraham live
in tents. He was looking for '*a city which hath foun-*
dations, whose builder and maker is God' (Hebrews
11:10). It was this faith that propelled Moses to forsake
the momentary pleasure of being a prince in Egypt. He
identified with God's people and endured, because he

saw *'him who is invisible'* (Hebrews 11:27). It was
this faith that made Paul the apostle endure much
persecution and deprivation with great joy, concluding
that, *'Our light affliction, which is but for a moment,
worketh for us a far more exceeding and eternal weight
of glory'* (II Corinthians 4:17).

We need to go beyond faith for salvation, faith for
daily living and faith for the miraculous and see beyond
the veil of the natural. Our faith must grasp the eternal
realities of the glory of heaven reserved for us. This will
bring a dimension of spiritual depth to our lives. We
will find ourselves not living for time but for eternity.
We will not be living for the present glory which fades
but for the eternal glory reserved for us in heaven. We
will not be living for ourselves, but for God and for
the Lord Jesus Christ. We will endure persecutions
with joy, we will labour for souls with gladness, we
will count every sacrifice for Jesus and His Kingdom
a privilege, and martyrdom will be a honour. How we
need this dimension of faith in these days of instant
success.

A Faith That Grows And Grows!

Just as there are people who have no faith, there are
others with little faith. These are those who worry
daily about how they will eat, what to wear and the
like. Jesus our Lord, in speaking about this, said,

> *Wherefore, if God so clothe the grass of the field,
> which today is, and tomorrow is cast into the oven,
> shall he not much more clothe you, O ye of little
> faith?*

(Matthew 6:30)

He, therefore, urged us not to worry and fret about the
issues of life but to trust God that He will take care of
us and meet our needs. He said that as we put first His
Kingdom and His righteousness, all other things shall
be added unto us.

> *Therefore take no thought, saying, What shall we*
> *eat? or, What shall we drink? or, Wherewithal*
> *shall we be clothed? ... But seek ye first the*
> *kingdom of God, and his righteousness; and all*
> *these things shall be added unto you.*
>
> (Matthew 6:31,33)

We are to have a living faith that is active, effective,
dynamic and prevailing. It may be as small as a mus-
tard seed, yet so powerful it moves mountains and
fills up every valley. This is not dead but living faith.
Though small, yet not little. Dynamic and effective.
That is what your faith should be.

If it is a living faith, then it should grow. It moves
from one stage to another. It is like a little child. There
is a time it can only sit up, it cannot move around. As
days go by, it begins to crawl all over the house. Later
it starts to walk, with a stagger. Then it is steady and
can walk and run and jump. This is how your faith
should grow. There was a time I could only believe
God to supply us a maximum of N2,000 a month for
ministry work. Whenever that happened we would
rejoice and celebrate the goodness of the Lord. Now
a major crusade or even a building project can cost us
some millions of naira, and God supplies the money
by faith. Sometime ago, I could only believe God for a
crowd of 500 people at a crusade service. Whenever a
crowd of about 100 people gave their lives to the Lord
we truly had a landslide! Now we can have over 200,000

in a single crusade service – drawn by the mighty hand of God, by faith. When you are in possession of a living faith, it will grow. Growth is one of the characteristics of living things.

This was the case with the Thessalonian brethren. When they heard the Gospel message, they were soundly converted. They turned from every sin and idol with all of their hearts unto the true and living God. They received the word of the Gospel, not the Word of God. Even though they faced so much persecution on account of their Christian faith, yet they moved on steadily and their faith grew increasingly. Paul had this to say about them.

We are bound to thank God always for you, brethren, as it is meet, because that your faith groweth exceedingly, and the charity of every one of you all toward each other aboundeth; so that we ourselves glory in you in the churches of God for your patience and faith in all your persecutions and tribulations that ye endure.

(II Thessalonians 1:3–4)

Your faith groweth exceedingly! I like that. I want my faith to grow exceedingly, that I may be increasingly profitable for the Kingdom of God. That should be your aspiration – that your faith should grow exceedingly. Then it will produce more results and bring greater glory to God.

Faith Food

If faith is going to grow then it must be nurtured and fed. And the main food of faith is the Word of God. '*So then faith cometh by hearing, and hearing by the word of God'* (Romans 10:17).

Faith comes by hearing the Word of God. Faith grows by feeding it with the Word of God. If your faith is going to grow, you must feed it with the word of faith.

The word that will feed faith must be positive, strong, balanced teachings of the Scriptures under the anointing of the Holy Spirit. There are some teachings that breed fear, doubt and unbelief. These are teachings that focus on the devil and his works. There are teachings that focus on men. These will not feed your faith. You have to watch what you read and hear if your faith is to be healthy and strong. Teachings that do not exalt and glorify Jesus, nor inspire confidence in the abilities of God to perform miracles, must be avoided like the plague. The warning of the Scriptures is clear on this:

To the law and to the testimony: if they speak not according to this word, it is because there is no light in them.

(Isaiah 8:20)

Cease, my son, to hear the instruction that causeth to err from the words of knowledge.

(Proverbs 19:27)

On a daily basis, therefore, feed your faith with a solid intake of the undiluted Word of God. The Scriptures must be read and digested daily. As you meditate on the Word of God, your faith will grow. Invest in good quality literature and tapes. Read and be wise; listen and be enlightened. If you receive the strong meat of the Word of God, you will live thereby. Jesus said, *'Man shall not live by bread alone, but by every word that proceedeth out of the mouth of God'* (Matthew 4:4).

Above all, find a Bible-believing church, that has a Spirit-filled man as the pastor, and identify fully with that assembly. Attend the services regularly, and receive the teachings of the Word of God. This is one of the ways by which your faith will grow.

Finally, take time to exercise your faith. If it is not put to work, it will soon be dead. Put it to work daily. Dare to believe God. Dare to act on His Word of promise. Dare to build your life on the Word. Dare to live by faith, for *'the just shall live by his faith'* (Habakkuk 2:2).

Chapter Fifteen
The Weapon Of Praise

Praise is a mighty weapon of spiritual warfare that we really need to know about and make use of. God has provided us with this weapon which Satan has always found irresistible. It is a weapon that breaks the back of Satan more than anything else.

We are commanded in the Scriptures to enter into intimate fellowship with God, through praise. *'Enter into his gates with thanksgiving, and into his courts with praise: be thankful unto him, and bless his name'* (Psalm 100:4). Immediately we start to worship and praise the Lord in the spirit, we enter into a deep communion with Him. There is a flow of divine life into us that gives us strength for the battle of life and fills us with great confidence and boldness. We, being in the spirit of worship, therefore, can begin to pour out our hearts to Him in effectual fervent prayer that cannot fail to produce results. The way to effective and intimate fellowship with the Lord is through praise. If you are rich in praise-worship with the Lord, your prayer life will be powerful, your faith will be very strong and your spiritual life will be very deep.

Jesus Christ has made every believer a priest of God.

Unto him that loved us, and washed us from our sins in his own blood, and hath made us kings and

*priests unto God and his Father; to him be glory
and dominion for ever and ever. Amen.*

(Revelation 1:5–6)

*But ye are a chosen generation, a royal priesthood,
an holy nation, a peculiar people; that ye should
shew forth the praises of him who hath called you
out of darkness into his marvellous light.*

(I Peter 2:9)

As God's priests, we are to offer to Him a daily sacrifice
of worship and praise. I believe the first duty of every
believer each morning, as he is getting out of bed,
should be to give God quality worship and praise, from
the depth of the heart. This is how to give each day a
victorious start. But the devil will always want to divert
us from our priestly ministry. He will want us to rob
God of the worship due to Him. That is why he often
brings heaviness, sorrows, difficulties and things that
can divert us from really praising the Lord. We should
not allow him to. Let us be determined – God must
have the glory due to His name. By the Holy Spirit
and through Jesus Christ let us offer to God a regular
and consistent sacrifice of praise.

*By him therefore let us offer the sacrifice of praise
to God continually, that is, the fruit of our lips
giving thanks to his name.*

(Hebrews 13:15)

Victory Through Praise

We are commanded to wage an effective spiritual warfare against the powers of darkness through praise.
Praise, the Word of God says, will bind the enemies

and keep them paralysed. Every saint is expected to
participate in this. God has ordained certain victory
for us over the princes of darkness through praise.

Let the saints be joyful in glory:
Let them sing aloud upon their beds.
Let the high praises of God be in their mouth,
And a two-edged sword in their hand;
To execute vengeance upon the heathen,
And punishments upon the people;
To bind their kings with chains,
And their nobles with fetters of iron;
To execute upon them the judgment written:
This honour have all his saints.
     Praise ye the LORD.

                              (Psalm 149:5–9)

The devil may lay a siege against you, his demons may
have been sent to work against you – at work, at home,
in your family or even in your body. Take up your weapons – the two-edged sword which is the Word of God
in your hand, the high praises of God in your mouth.
As you begin to praise and worship the Lord, your
victory will come. This is exactly what Jehoshaphat,
king of Judah did. Three great nations came against
him in battle: the children of Ammon, Moab and Mount
Seir. Instead of running away, the king turned to the
Lord in prayer and fasting (he himself and the whole
nation). In his prayer before the people, he confessed
their helplessness to the Lord, saying

For we have no might against this great company
that cometh against us; neither know we what to
do: but our eyes are upon thee.

                         (II Chronicles 20:12)

When he had finished praying, the Spirit of the Lord came upon Jahaziel the son of Zechariah and he prophesied: *'Ye shall not need to fight in this battle: set yourselves, stand ye still, and see the salvation of the LORD with you'*, (II Chronicles 20:17).

Jehoshaphat obeyed the command of the Lord and set the people in array, not to fight but to worship the Lord and to praise Him in the beauty of holiness. As they did this the power of darkness moving the enemies was bound and the Lord gave them victory.

> *And when they began to sing and to praise, the LORD set ambushments against the children of Ammon, Moab, and mount Seir, which were come against Judah; and they were smitten.*
>
> (II Chronicles 20:22)

Our warfare is not against flesh and blood, but against spiritual forces. They hate worship and praise to the most high God and are most easily routed with this weapon. Therefore, when the battle seems toughest, apply the weapon of praise. You will break the backbone of the enemy.

Turning A Hopeless Situation Around

With the weapon of praise we can turn a seemingly hopeless situation around for God.

Paul and Silas were faithful servants of God. But they were arrested and beaten for preaching the Gospel. Backs aching, feet in sores, stomachs empty, they were shut up inside a dark dungeon. No preacher could have it worse. They could have murmured and grumbled.

They could have decided never to preach the Gospel again. But, instead, they praised God.

> *And at midnight Paul and Silas prayed, and sang praises unto God: and the prisoners heard them. And suddenly there was a great earthquake, so that the foundations of the prison were shaken: and immediately all the doors were opened, and every one's bands were loosed.*
>
> (Acts 16:25–26)

Praising God at midnight in prison, when it was really dark and gloomy? Yes, that was the sure way to victory. Had they not employed the weapon of praise, that could have been the end of their missionary career. But praises brought the Almighty God onto the scene. There was an earthquake; the foundations of the prison shook. The doors were opened, their chains fell off. Praises can shake open the doors of your 'prisons' where the enemy has got you trapped. Praises can break all your fetters and set you free. The time when all hope seems lost and it appears you are trapped, that is the time to praise the Lord from the depth of your heart. Surely it is a great sacrifice praising Him at such a time. But that is the exact sacrifice the Lord is pleased with.

> *And let them sacrifice the sacrifices of*
>   *thanksgiving,*
> *And declare his works with rejoicing.*
>
> (Psalm 107:22)

> *By him therefore let us offer the sacrifice of praise to God continually, that is, the fruit of our lips giving thanks to his name.*
>
> (Hebrews 13:15)

It costs something to really praise the Lord when you do not feel like doing it, but it really works. Permit me to draw a parallel here between the weapon of prayer and that of praise.

When Peter was imprisoned, according to the Bible the whole Church prayed for him fervently and continuously. *'Peter therefore was kept in prison: but prayer was made without ceasing of the church unto God for him'* (Acts 12:5).

The Lord responded to the fervent prayers of the Church by sending an angel down to deliver Peter out of captivity. But when Paul and Silas were put in prison, the two of them prayed and sang praises to God. The Lord responded to the heartfelt worship of these His faithful ministers by coming down personally Himself, causing that earthquake that broke the prison doors open. Surely, the Almighty God inhabits the praises of His people (Psalm 22:3).

Once we were to hold a programme on a university campus. It had been much publicised, and the people of God had laboured and prayed relentlessly. We were looking forward to a bountiful harvest of souls. However, on the night preceding the crusade, the Students' Union issued a statement saying that no meeting, rally or gathering should be held for a week, as from that night, because of a special students programme. They threatened to disturb such a meeting if it were held. Being the President of the Christian Union, I was greatly concerned. All contact failed to yield anything positive. After a time of agonising prayer, the Spirit led me to begin to praise the Lord. As I was praising Him a deep peace and strong confidence flooded my soul. I knew that all was well and I went round to encourage the brethren.

The meeting commenced the following night with a

huge crowd. The visiting evangelist had an unusual anointing and liberty. The Students' Union, in keeping with their word sent a delegation to interrupt our meeting. But on seeing the huge crowd those students merely took their seats at the rear of the auditorium, waiting for a convenient time to act. The Holy Spirit arrested them, however, and some of them went forward in response to the altar call. This is what praise can do.

What makes praise so powerful a weapon against the enemy? God is in the midst of the praises of His people. Praising God therefore, involves God in that matter and the omnipotent power of the Almighty is released. *'But thou art holy, O thou that inhabitest the praises of Israel'* (Psalm 22:3).

Praise is prayer's most powerful ally. But it is not just an ally, it is an important element of prayer. The prayer that is effective is not just the one offered with strong supplications but also with heartfelt praise to God.

> *Be careful for nothing; but in every thing by prayer and supplication with thanksgiving let your requests be made known unto God.*
>
> (Philippians 4:6)

Praises In All Things

We are to give thanks to God in everything. There are people who always see the devil in everything that happens. They never see God in anything, working for their good. They always see the negative, talk the

negative, think the negative, and believe the negative.
Eventually they get ensnared by the words of their
mouths. They are always sad, looking miserable and
as if all hope is lost. But what does Scripture say?

Rejoice in the Lord alway: and again I say, Rejoice.
                                                (Philippians 4:4)

*And whatsoever ye do in word or deed, do all in
the name of the Lord Jesus, giving thanks to God
and the Father by him.*

                                                (Colossians 3:17)

*In everything give thanks: for this is the will of
God in Christ Jesus concerning you.*
                                                (I Thessalonians 5:18)

Please note that the Scriptures say: 'in everything',
'always' and 'in whatsoever ye do', we should praise
the Lord, give thanks to Him, and rejoice in His
name. Our service, and our labour for Him should
be joyfully done. The people of Israel came under
judgment because although they enjoyed great benefits,
they were not thankful.

*Because thou servedst not the LORD thy God with
joyfulness, and with gladness of heart, for the
abundance of all things; therefore shalt thou serve
thine enemies which the LORD shall send against
thee, in hunger, and in thirst, and in nakedness,
and in want of all things.*

                                                (Deuteronomy 28:47–48)

Let us learn from this and take warning.
   The way to win the battle of life at all times is by
living in constant worship and praise. The life of David,

king of Israel, exemplified this. Possibly no man saw greater conflicts – spiritual, physical, domestic and political. But for the case of Bathsheba, Uriah's wife, he won all of his battles. Even the one he lost was sufficient to have knocked him out of the race altogether. But he genuinely repented before the Lord. Never again were these sins mentioned in connection with him. The secret was in his ability to praise the Lord at all times. He made a quality decision to bless the Lord always. And come what may, David was a winner anytime.

> *I will bless the LORD at all times:*
> *His praise shall continually be in my mouth.*
> *My soul shall make her boast in the LORD:*
> *The humble shall hear thereof, and be glad.*
>   (Psalm 34:1–2)

> *I will sing of the mercies of the LORD for ever:*
> *With my mouth will I make known thy*
>   *faithfulness to all generations.*
>   (Psalm 89:1)

Worship is a means of spiritual growth and edification. Watch an individual who takes time to personally give God quality praises and adoration – he will grow rapidly and have constant divine manifestations. In like manner, churches, assemblies and fellowships where effective worship in songs, music or the word of mouth are encouraged, grow rapidly and have the divine power of God in constant manifestation in their midst. Paul Billheimer, in his excellent book, *Destined For the Throne*, remarks that investigations reveal that the most rapidly growing Christian denominations are those that make effective spontaneous and joyful worship a prominent feature of their activities. To a large extent, he is correct. Worship is powerful. It ushers you right into the presence of God. It breaks prison doors open, and it makes spiritual growth rapid. Take time to cultivate the habit of worship and praise.

Our ability to worship God effectively depends upon our meditation in His Word and our complete reliance on the Holy Spirit.

Our concept and understanding of God will greatly enhance our appreciation of Him which is expressed in worship. If we are shallow in knowledge, our worship will be superficial. But, if we really know Him our worship will be deep. Hence, the great need to meditate on the greatness and the majesty of God, which is revealed in nature as well as in His Word.

Much more than this, the Holy Spirit will help us worship God as we should. We are limited but He is not. When we depend on Him and allow Him to take over our worship it will be deep and profound, a mighty weapon in spiritual warfare. Our worship must be in the spirit. This is not just limited to worshipping in an unknown tongue. It only means we have to be in the spirit and not in the flesh, propelled and energised and inspired by the Spirit of the Lord as we worship Him. Effective worship is done in the spirit and in truth. *'God is a Spirit: and they that worship him must worship him in spirit and in truth'* (John 4:24).

In concluding this chapter it is worth noting that *'the dead praise not the LORD'* (Psalm 115:17). The Bible here is not talking about those who are dead physically. Abraham is dead physically but he is alive in heaven, praising and worshipping the Lord. Likewise, Paul and all the other saints that have passed on to their reward. They are not really dead, they are alive. Those who are dead are those who have not been born again. Dead spiritually. Dead in trespasses and sin. Far away from God – such cannot praise the Lord in the true sense of

praise. They need to come alive. They need to repent
and be born again. They need to sincerely accept Christ
as their Saviour and Lord. You ought to lay hold of these
weapons and fight the good fight of faith. Are you really
alive and well spiritually? Then let all that is within you
praise His holy name.

> *Bless the LORD, O my soul:*
> *And all that is within me, bless his holy name.*
> *Bless the LORD, O my soul,*
> *And forget not all his benefits.*
>
> (Psalm 103:1–2)

If you have not been born again at all, what you have
been reading is the Lord speaking to you. Repent
sincerely and give your heart to Jesus. Then, you
will really begin to live and praise the Lord. God
Himself will start to work with you confirming His
Word in diverse ways. With God working with you,
you are more than a conqueror.

> *Beloved . . . it was needful for me to write unto*
> *you, and exhort you that ye should earnestly*
> *contend for the faith which was once delivered*
> *unto the saints.*
>
> (Jude 3)

Chapter Sixteen
The Power of Unity

*Behold, how good and how pleasant it is for
brethren to dwell together in unity!*

(Psalm 133:1)

Unity is a vital weapon of spiritual warfare that we
cannot do without these days. To win a decisive
victory over the adversary we need to join hands
with other believers and *'fight the good fight of faith'*
together. Paul the apostle said: *'For we wrestle not
against flesh and blood, but against principalities,
against powers'* (Ephesians 6:12). *'We wrestle not'*, not
'I wrestle not'. That underlines the necessity of unity.
Effective spiritual warfare is best done collectively. We
are to join our hearts and hands and present a common
front against the adversary. That is how the Kingdom
of God will advance.

In spiritual warfare, our strength is multiplied as we
unite. Whereas one can put a thousand to flight, two
will effectively put ten thousand to flight; according
to God's Word. Standing alone can prove suicidal,
whereas there are greater results and rewards in
unity. The Bible clearly says that two are better than
one. This is never more so than in spiritual warfare.

There is one alone, and there is not a second;

yea, he hath neither child nor brother: yet is there no end of all his labour; neither is his eye satisfied with riches; neither saith he, For whom do I labour, and bereave my soul of good? This is also vanity, yea, it is a sore travail. Two are better than one; because they have a good reward for their labour. For if they fall, the one will lift up his fellow: but woe to him that is alone when he falleth; for he hath not another to help him up. Again, if two lie together, then they have heat: but how can one be warm alone? And if one prevail against him, two shall withstand him; and a threefold cord is not quickly broken.

(Ecclesiastes 4:8–12)

In the scriptures quoted above, clear reasons are given why two are better than one.

First, for better and greater result, *'have a good reward for their labour'*. In these days of accelerated evangelism when all plans are to ensure maximum impact for the Gospel before the return of the Lord, unity is a factor that will greatly multiply our result. Spiritual assistance, encouragement and mutual edification is a product of unity.

No one can stand alone successfully. As human beings, there are times of weariness and discouragement. We are to lift up one another – *'woe to him that is alone when he falleth; for he hath not another to help him up'*. This is the undoing of many leaders, especially those who are so outstandingly gifted that they think they can stand alone. You are part of a body. You are to function in agreement with other parts of the body. It is when the enemy wants to devastate a man that he lures him to separate himself from the brethren and stand alone.

Next, for fellowship. We are to warm one another. Although this speaks primarily of marriage, it also applies spiritually. We can provoke and inspire one another to love and to good works.

For victory. It is as we stand together that we are able to withstand and overcome the adversary. This is to let us know how crucial unity is in spiritual warfare. Pay attention to it.

I have seen ministers operate in isolation as though other members of the body of Christ are irrelevant. They soon find out that they cannot go far. If we are going to last in the service of the Kingdom, we must walk in unity with other members of the body of Christ, as much as possible.

Negatively Employed

The Bible gives an account of how the power of unity was negatively employed by the people just before the flood of Noah.

God had said that they should spread over the earth. But these folks said they would not. They decided to build a tower of Babel, a tower of rebellion, that would reach to heaven, a proud monument in their memory. And they were united in their purpose. They were of one language, of one accord.

> And the whole earth was of one language, and of one speech. And it came to pass, as they journeyed from the east, that they found a plain in the land of Shinar; and they dwelt there. And they said one to another, Go to, let us make brick, and burn them thoroughly. And they had brick for stone, and slime had they for morter. And they said, Go to,

let us build us a city and a tower, whose top may reach unto heaven; and let us make us a name, lest we be scattered abroad upon the face of the whole earth.

(Genesis 11:1—4)

When the Lord came down to see what they were doing, He commented on their unity and acknowledged that there was nothing they wanted to do there that they could not do. That is the power of unity.

And the LORD said, Behold, the people is one, and they have all one language; and this they begin to do: and now nothing will be restrained from them, which they have imagined to do. Go to, let us go down, and there confound their language, that they may not understand one another's speech. So the LORD scattered them abroad from thence upon the face of all the earth: and they left off to build the city.

(Genesis 11:6—8)

How I wish those folks had been united in obedience to God. They could then have accomplished their heart's desire.

There God Commanded His Blessings

It is in the place of unity that God's blessings flow, unhindered. When believers truly agree together, there is no force in existence to stop the flow of divine blessing. That is why it is good and pleasant for brethren to live together in unity. That is why we are to endeavour to keep the unity of Spirit in the bond of peace. There is nothing you do to keep the unity of the Spirit that is too much.

> *Behold, how good and how pleasant it is*
> *For brethren to dwell together in unity!*
> *It is like the precious ointment upon the head,*
> *That ran down upon the beard,*
> *Even Aaron's beard:*
> *That went down to the skirts of his garments;*
> *As the dew of Hermon,*
> *And as the dew that descended upon the*
> *   mountains of Zion:*
> *For there the Lord commanded the blessing,*
> *Even life for evermore.*
>
> (Psalm 133)

That God commands His blessings where there is unity is clearly demonstrated in the book of the Acts of the Apostles. The Church was young and God showed in a practical way how He wanted the Church to function. After the Lord Jesus rose and ascended into heaven, the believers came together to pray. How did they pray?

> *These all continued with one accord in prayer*
> *and supplication, with the women, and Mary the*
> *mother of Jesus, and with his brethren.*
>
> (Acts 1:14)

Because they prayed in one accord, they operated with great power. They were simply fulfilling the Word of our Lord Jesus Christ.

> *Verily I say unto you, Whatsoever ye shall bind on*
> *earth shall be bound in heaven: and whatsoever*

ye shall loose on earth shall be loosed in heaven.
Again I say unto you, That if two of you shall agree
on earth as touching any thing that they shall ask,
it shall be done for them of my Father which is
in heaven. For where two or three are gathered
together in my name, there am I in the midst of
them.

(Matthew 18:18–20)

The early Church continued to pray, and they eventually received the Holy Spirit.

'*And when the day of Pentecost was fully come, they*
were all with one accord in one place' (Acts 2:1).

This is indeed a church getting ready for effective
spiritual warfare. The reason why churches are not
very effective these days is because there is no unity.
We are divided and the enemy uses this to weaken us.
Going further into the history of the early Church the
Bible says that they continued steadfastly in unity.

And they continued steadfastly in the apostles'
doctrine and fellowship, and in breaking of bread,
and in prayers. And fear came upon every soul:
and many wonders and signs were done by the
apostles. And all that believed were together, and
had all things common; and sold their possessions
and goods, and parted them to all men, as every
man had need. And they, continuing daily with
one accord in the temple, and breaking bread
from house to house, did eat their meat with
gladness and singleness of heart, praising God,
and having favour with all the people. And the
Lord added to the church daily such as should be
saved.

(Acts 2:42–47)

*And being let go, they went to their own company,
and reported all that the chief priests and elders
had said unto them. And when they heard that, they
lifted up their voice to God with one accord, and
said, Lord, thou art God, which hast made heaven,
and earth, and the sea, and all that in them is.*

(Acts 4:23–24)

*And now, Lord, behold their threatenings: and
grant unto thy servants, that with all boldness
they may speak thy word, by stretching forth thine
hand to heal; and that signs and wonders may be
done by the name of thy holy child Jesus.*

*And when they had prayed, the place was
shaken where they were assembled together; and
they were all filled with the Holy Ghost, and
they spake the word of God with boldness. And
the multitude of them that believed were of one
heart and of one soul: neither said any of them
that ought of the things which he possessed was
his own; but they had all things common. And
with great power gave the apostles witness of the
resurrection of the Lord Jesus: and great grace was
upon them all. Neither was there any among them
that lacked: for as many as were possessors of
lands or houses sold them, and brought the prices
of the things that were sold.*

(Acts 4:29–34)

Do you see how the Church was? Because they were
united, they grew. Their prayers were answered. They
were filled with the Holy Spirit. They preached the
Word with great power. There were signs and miracles
and all their needs were met. God can do it again. If
we will bring down the walls of separation, if we will

build bridges and reach out to one another, if we will truly unite, then we shall see God's power at work again as in the days of old and His blessings shall flow in abundance. It is in the place of unity that God commands His blessings.

Bringing Down The Glory

When the Temple of Solomon was being dedicated, the glory of God came and filled it. Individually, you and I are the temple of the Holy Spirit. Collectively, we are the house, the holy habitation of the Lord. What the Lord did with the temple in the Old Testament, He wants to do with you and I individually, and with the Church collectively. We are to be vessels – filled and covered with His glory. But lets see how the glory came upon Solomon's temple.

> *Now when the priests came out of the holy place (for all the priests who were present had sanctified themselves, without regard to their divisions; and all the Levitical singers, Asaph, Heman, and Jeduthun, their sons and kinsmen, arrayed in fine linen, with cymbals, harps, and lyres, stood east of the altar with a hundred and twenty priests who were trumpeters; and it was the duty of the trumpeters and singers to make themselves heard in unison in praise and thanksgiving to the LORD, and when the song was raised, with trumpets and cymbals and other musical instruments, in praise to the LORD,*
> *"For he is good,*
>   *for his steadfast love endures for ever,"*

*the house, the house of the LORD, was filled with
a cloud, so that the priests could not stand to
minister because of the cloud; for the glory of the
LORD filled the house of God.*

(II Chronicles 5:11–14, RSV)

It was as the singers were united as one in worship and
praise that the glory of the Lord came down. It was so
real that none of the priests could stand on their feet –
they all fell under the anointing. Where there is unity
of the Spirit in worship, the glory will appear and the
people will be blessed.

In The Unity Of Faith

The unity of the Spirit among believers is something
we should work and pray for. It was a central theme in
the prayer of our Lord Jesus Christ shortly before He
left for heaven. He prayed, *'that they may be one, as
we are'* (John 17:11, 21–23). Jesus, who taught against
vain repetition in prayer, mentioned our being one, four
different times within a short space of time. Was he
guilty of vain repetition? No, He was only strongly
expressing the burden of His heart and His passionate
desire to see believers come together in unity. He knew
that when we are united we can do much more for the
Kingdom. He said that our unity will demonstrate to
the world that He is actually from the Father.

*'And now I am no more in the world, but they are
in the world, and I am coming to thee. Holy Father,
keep them in thy name, which thou has given me,
that they may be one, even as we are one.'*

(John 17:11, RSV)

'Even as thou, Father, art in me, and I in thee,
that they also may be in us, so that the world may
believe that thou hast sent me. The glory which
thou hast given me I have given to them, that they
may be one even as we are one, I in them and thou
in me, that they may become perfectly one, so that
the world may know that thou hast sent me and
hast loved them even as thou hast loved me.'

(John 17:21–23, RSV)

When you walk in unity with other members of the
body of Christ you are actually fulfilling in it the strong
desires of our Lord Jesus Christ.

Paul the apostle, too, taught and laboured to establish the saints in unity. It was a passion of his heart
and life. It was to him the Lord gave the understanding
of the Church as the body of Christ. Even though there
are many members and parts of that body, it is still
one body.

I therefore, a prisoner for the Lord, beg you to lead
a life worthy of the calling to which you have
been called, with all lowliness and meekness, with
patience, forbearing one another in love, eager to
maintain the unity of the Spirit in the bond of
peace. There is one body and one Spirit, just as
you were called to the one hope that belongs to
your call, one Lord, one faith, one baptism, one
God and Father of us all, who is above all and
through all and in all.

(Ephesians 4:1–6, RSV)

For just as the body is one and has many members,
and all the members of the body, though many, are
one body, so it is with Christ. For by one Spirit we

> *were all baptized into one body – Jews or Greeks,*
> *slaves or free – and all were made to drink of one*
> *Spirit.*
>
> *For the body does not consist of one member but*
> *of many.*
>
> (I Corinthians 12:12–14, RSV)

Here he taught us to walk in lowliness and long-suffering and to endure and forbear with one another. He made it very clear that there is the one body of Christ. He went on to mention some of the things that unite us.

- We belong to one body – the same body.
- We have one Lord – the Lord Jesus Christ.
- We share one faith – the faith of our Lord Jesus.
- We have one God and Father.
- There is one baptism – by the body of Christ.
- We share in the one Holy Spirit.
- We are going to the same heaven.

Why then can't we agree to love one another? We do not necessarily have to bear the same name or belong to the same denomination or the same movements. So long as we are born again, and filled with the Holy Spirit, we are members of the same body. You can argue with it but you can do nothing about it. You have no choice whatever. Why then can't we begin to walk in unity and love, helping one another, joining our hands to advance God's Kingdom. That was the argument of Paul. It was the passion of his life.

> *So if there is any encouragement in Christ, any*
> *incentive of love, any participation in the Spirit,*

any affection and sympathy, complete my joy by being of the same mind, having the same love, being in full accord and of one mind. Do nothing from self- ishness or conceit, but in humility count others bet- ter than yourselves. Let each of you look not only to his own interests, but also to the interests of others.
                              (Philippians 2:1–4, RSV)

For I want you to know how greatly I strive for you, and for those at Laodicea, and for all who have not seen my face, that their hearts may be encouraged as they are knit together in love, to have all the riches of assured understanding and the knowledge of God's mystery, of Christ, in whom are hid all the treasures of wisdom and knowledge.
                              (Colossians 2:1–3, RSV)

We are to be of one spirit, of one accord. We are to be knitted together in love and to grow up together into the fullness of the stature of Christ. Throughout his life-time Paul laboured to promote the unity of the body of Christ.

Unity Under Attack

There is nothing the enemy hates as much as the unity of the body of Christ. He knows that if he can keep us divided, opposing one another, he will keep us busy dissipating our spiritual energy on irrelevances, while he is busy devastating the harvest field.

Our Lord Jesus warned us against the devices of the devil and we must not be ignorant of these devices.

Knowing their thoughts, he said to them, 'Every kingdom divided against itself is laid waste, and no city or house divided against itself will stand.'
                                    (Matthew 12:25, RSV)

There have been many strong movements of the Holy Spirit that died out on the platform of division and strife. Churches that ought to have become strong and influential have been terribly weakened through strife, division and disunity. There have been fractions, breakaways and rifts, especially in pentecostal churches. This is not God's perfect will. He is not the author of confusion and strife. It is the devil that is responsible for division. Divide and rule is the game of the devil. There is no move of the Holy Spirit that the devil would not want to attack. One of his principal weapons is division. As soon as the early Church began to grow, Satan came with his tricks.

Now in these days when the disciples were increasing in number, the Hellenists murmured against the Hebrews because their widows were neglected in the daily distribution.

                                          (Acts 6:1, RSV)

That is the enemy waiting to quench the fire of the Holy Spirit. But the apostles handled it right. They set themselves to pray. They applied the Word of God. They set up deacons to serve and take care of the needs of those who felt neglected. Through divine wisdom they quenched the fire of strife the enemy had kindled. The result? Growth in every dimension. It is always the case when the people of God do not allow the enemy to cause division. '*And the word of God increased; and the number of the disciples multiplied greatly in Jerusalem, and a great many of the priests were obedient to the faith'* (Acts 6:7, RSV).

As soon as the early Church embarked on mission, the devil came again with strife, this time within the leadership. Paul and Barnabas were in such sharp disagreement they eventually parted ways. If that matter had not been handled with care and maturity it would have ended the missionary effort of the Church.

> *And there arose a sharp contention, so that they separated from each other; Barnabas took Mark with him and sailed away to Cyprus, but Paul chose Silas and departed, being commended by the brethren to the grace of the Lord. And he went through Syria and Cilicia, strengthening the churches.*
>
> (Acts 15:39–41, RSV)

In the scripture above, Barnabas took Mark and went into Cyprus, but Paul chose Silas and they were commended to the grace of God by the Church. If you have to leave a church or a ministry to go into something new God is asking you to do, you must not cause any strife or division; you must not go in a hurry, but wait to be commended to the grace of God. God never blesses rebelliousness; with a little patience you can go with the full blessing of God's people. And that will make a difference in your life and service for God. It is worth noting that after this episode Barnabas never features prominantly again in the New Testament, whereas Paul is in the forefront of biblical accounts of the work of God in the Early Church. Why? One was commended to the grace of God by the Church, and the other just went out on his own. Don't just go. Wait and be commended to the grace of God by His people.

Let There Be Unity

One of the key things the Holy Spirit wants to accomplish in these end-times is to secure the unity of God's people. But it involves the co-operation of each member of the body of Christ.

A close look at the Scriptures shows what it will take. We have to pray for it, we have to work at it and we must not give up.

> *For just as the body is one and has many members, and all the members of the body, though many, are one body, so it is with Christ. For by one Spirit we were all baptized into one body – Jews or Greeks, slaves or free – and all were made to drink of one Spirit.*
>
> (I Corinthians 12:12–13, RSV)

In the above scripture we are made to know that there is only one body of Christ. We, although different faces and races, are all members of the same body. Our giftings and callings may be different but we are members of the same body. Each one of us occupies a unique place in the body of Christ. Some are like the eye, some like the foot, some like the ear. We are organically related and spiritually dependent. None of us can truly stand alone without the other members of the body. We need one another. *'The eye cannot say unto the hand, I have no need of thee: nor again the head to the feet, I have no need of you'* (I Corinthians 12:21). A knowledge of this makes us know and appreciate the other members of the body of Christ.

In order to walk in unity certain virtues are needed:

- Lowliness

- Meekness
- Longsuffering

We are to have the mind of Christ, seek to serve one another and esteem each other better than ourselves. In honour we are to prefer one another. That is what the Bible says (Philippians 2:3–4); and *'Be kindly affectioned one to another with brotherly love; in honour preferring one another'* (Romans 12:10).

These are the Christ-like virtues that will give birth to genuine unity of the Spirit. The absence of these is what is responsible for all the strife and problems we have in the Church today. There is so much competitiveness, pride and arrogance; there is so much showmanship and rivalry. All these breed strife, contention and division, but we must allow the Holy Spirit to work in our hearts, producing the humility and the virtue of Christ. You need to begin to see other believers in Christ as your brothers and sisters, and to walk in love. Together we shall use this weapon and prevail against the adversary.

Chapter Seventeen

That Thou Mightest War A Good Warfare

This book is not written just as an academic exercise. I have not written mere theology, or a theory. It is written with the full consciousness that we are daily involved in a battle.

> *For we wrestle not against flesh and blood, but against principalities, against powers, against the rulers of the darkness of this world, against spiritual wickedness in high places. Wherefore take unto you the whole armour God, that ye may be able to withstand in the evil day, and having done all, to stand.*
>
> (Ephesians 6:12–13)

These weapons, as discussed in this book are provided by our loving heavenly Father so that we may use them to '*fight the good fight of faith*', win the victory over the adversary and lay hold of eternal life. There is absolutely no reason for the devil to run you down. There is no reason for you to live in defeat, oppression and afflictions. Stand up in Jesus. Take up your weapons of war. Begin to apply them diligently, skillfully, and see how darkness gives way to light, defeat to victory, sickness to health and failure to success.

There is also the battle for the souls of men. The devil is trying his best to rule the world and keep men and women in bondage. But, we know that *'The earth is the LORD'S, and the fulness thereof; the world, and they that dwell therein'* (Psalm 24:1). We also know that Jesus is the rightful Lord of all mankind and that *'he must reign, till he hath put all enemies under his feet'* (I Corinthians 15:25). This actually is the core of our battle. After we have been liberated from the grip of the enemy, we are to labour relentlessly for the salvation of others. We are to employ these weapons of war to deal with Satan and all his hosts and release men and women from their grip. Paul had a clear understanding of this battle for the souls of men, and was fully involved in it. He used these God-appointed weapons fearlessly in order to release souls that Satan held captive, and to establish the lordship of Jesus Christ in the hearts of people and on earth. Writing to the Corinthians on this issue he said:

> *It is true that I am an ordinary, weak human being, but I don't use human plans and methods to win my battles. I use God's mighty weapons, not those made by men, to knock down the devil's strongholds. These weapons can break down every proud argument against God and every wall that can be built to keep men from finding him. With these weapons I can capture rebels and bring them back to God, and change them into men whose hearts' desire is obedience to Christ. I will use these weapons against every rebel who remains after I have first used them on you yourselves, and you surrender to Christ.*

> (II Corinthians 10:3–6, LB)

What boldness! What great confidence! What zeal for God, His Kingdom and His glory! Paul is a good example of how a soldier of Christ should employ the weapons of our warfare. These mighty weapons knock down the devil's strongholds; break down proud arguments built to keep men from knowing God; transform the hearts of rebels into saints of God. These definitely, are the works every believer should be doing. Everywhere you see the works of the devil they must be destroyed. Anywhere there are men bound in sin and satanic afflictions, they must be freed. Anywhere Satan poses as lord, he must be dethroned and the lordship of Jesus established. This charge Jesus gave us all and we are to zealously carry it out.

And he said unto them, Go ye into all the world, and preach the gospel to every creature. He that believeth and is baptized shall be saved; but he that believeth not shall be damned. And these signs shall follow them that believe; In my name shall they cast out devils; they shall speak with new tongues; they shall take up serpents; and if they drink any deadly thing, it shall not hurt them; they shall lay hands on the sick, and they shall recover.

(Mark 16:15–18)

Then he called his twelve disciples together, and gave them power and authority over all devils, and to cure diseases. And he sent them to preach the kingdom of God, and to heal the sick.

(Luke 9:1–2)

But ye shall receive power, after that the Holy Ghost is come upon you: and ye shall be witnesses unto me both in Jerusalem, and in all Judaea, and in Samaria, and unto the uttermost parts of the earth.

(Acts 1:8)

These are the battle charges. Our Lord has sent us, fully armed, to go into the world to liberate men and women from sin, sickness, ignorance, poverty and aatanic bondage and oppression, and from everlasting destruction. If you are truly born again, you should be a part of the Great Commission. You have the charge already and you have all the weapons of war at your disposal.

Do not be like Ephraim. *'The children of Ephraim, being armed, and carrying bows, Turned back in the day of battle'* (Psalm 78:9). Fear should not hold you back. Neither should you be preoccupied with worldly problems. Be involved in the battle of the Lord. Be among those that contend earnestly for the faith once delivered unto the saints. God bless you. This actually is the key reason for writing this book. To make sure you know what mighty weapons God has put at our disposal, to stir you up to lay hold of these weapons and fight the good fight of faith. Now that you know, you are responsible; knowledge brings responsibility. God now expects you to do something with what you know. As you step out in faith and in the Spirit to act on His Word, God Himself will start to work with you, confirming His Word in diverse ways. With God working with you, you are more than a conqueror.

Beloved, . . . it was needful for me to write unto you, and exhort you that ye should earnestly contend for the faith which was once delivered unto the saints.

(Jude 3)

Chapter Eighteen
I Am With You Always

There is one glorious fact that makes our victory in spiritual warfare certain. We are not only provided with adequate weapons, but the Lord Himself, who is the Victor of Calvary, the King of kings and the Lord of lords, is with us. He has promised never to leave us alone, and that makes our victory sure. *'And, lo, I am with you alway, even unto the end of the world. Amen'* (Matthew 28:20).

The abiding presence of the Lord is significant in the life of any human being. No man can truly succeed without it. No man can truly overcome Satan without it. No man can accomplish much for God without the divine presence. Throughout the Bible, and in contemporary history, one key factor for the success of men is the abiding presence of God. When God is there victory is sure. *'If God be for us, who can be against us?'* (Romans 8:31). The divine presence gives boldness for exploits.

Take Moses as an example. *'He endured as seeing him who is invisible'* (Hebrews 11:27). He did wonders in Egypt, led the Israelites across the Red Sea and the wilderness because God was with him. None of the adversaries could withstand Moses, because God was with Him. At one stage when the Lord decided to leave them because of their sins, he pleaded until God was pleased to go with them again. *'My presence shall go with thee'* the Lord promised, *'and I will give thee rest'* (Exodus 33:14). Begin to recognise and count on the abiding presence of the Most High with you; begin to practise the presence of God and it will make a whole lot of difference in your life. One of the key revelations that the Lord has used to sustain me in His service is that of His abiding presence. His promise to Joshua is so real to me, and I have had to claim it several times.

> *Have not I commanded thee? Be strong and of a good courage; be not afraid, neither be thou dismayed: for the LORD thy God is with thee whithersoever thou goest.*
>
> (Joshua 1:9)

Wherever you go! Anywhere. Anytime. Under every situation and in every circumstance – He is always there.

I remember some years ago, at the early stage of my ministry, I was invited to conduct a meeting at Agege, Lagos. Although I prepared for the meeting my expectation was not great. I thought it was to be attended by a few hundred. Unknown to me fourteen different churches had combined to get together a huge revival meeting and I was to be their guest speaker.

On arrival, I stayed in a pastor's office to relax and get prepared. At the time I was due to speak, I was taken to the venue. You can imagine my reaction as I saw a sea of heads – thousands of people, literally, and several men of God, most of whom were surprised that their guest speaker was so young (I was just twenty-nine years old then). Immediately, I stopped meditating on the message I had prepared and turned to Joshua 1:9, praying in the Spirit as I was claiming it. I was totally helpless. God had to do something. To make matters worse, the man who introduced me spoke in such a way that it seemed that if nothing special happened I was going to be in real trouble. I had to depend totally on the Lord. That night I preached on the law of sowing and reaping and it was abundantly evident that God was at work. Salvation in hundreds, healings, deliverances. There was such an unction upon me as I could not have produced had I prepared for months. God was at work confirming His abiding presence. Hudson Taylor once commented, 'All of God's giants have been weak men who did great things for God because they reckoned on God being with them.' Begin to count on the abiding presence of God and great things will begin to happen in your life.

It was the abiding presence of God that made Joseph a success, in spite of the various negative circumstances he met in life. The devil tried his best to stop him but the Lord was always there to give the comfort, assurance, joy and the victory he needed. That can also be your case.

Of David, this was written: '*And David went on, and grew great, and the* LORD *God of hosts was with him*' (II Samuel 5:10). The abiding presence of the Lord will cause you to go on, grow great, and succeed in the battle of life.

It was written of our Lord Jesus Christ:

How God anointed Jesus of Nazareth with the Holy Ghost and with power: who went about doing good, and healing all that were oppressed of the devil; for God was with him.

(Acts 10:38)

God was with Him. He was in perfect unity and fellowship with the Father. Hence, mighty signs and wonders manifested themselves. Through the abiding presence of God we can work the works that Christ worked, and even greater works. *'Verily, verily, I say unto you, He that believeth on me, the works that I do shall he do also; and greater works than these shall he do; because I go unto my Father'* (John 14:12).

When Paul was facing a crisis at Corinth, the Lord appeared to him and assured him of His abiding presence. That really gave the apostle great comfort, encouragement, and boldness to go on.

Then spake the Lord to Paul in the night by a vision, Be not afraid, but speak, and hold not thy peace: for I am with thee, and no man shall set on thee to hurt thee: for I have much people in this city.

(Acts 18:9–10)

During tough times, we need to count on the presence of the Lord, look to Him for help, and consciously and deliberately put the whole situation in His hands. Having done that, a miracle is inevitable.

God has also spoken concerning you and me. If you are truly born again, He has promised never to leave nor forsake you. You should, therefore, be strong and rejoice that God is with you wherever you go, whatever you may be doing. He is Jehovah-Shammah – the Lord who is ever present, Emmanuel – God with us.

Let your conversation be without covetousness; and be content with such things as ye have: for he hath said, I will never leave thee, nor forsake thee. So that we may boldly say,
   The Lord is my helper, and I will not fear
   What man shall do unto me.

(Hebrews 13:5–6)

Your first attitude to this promise is to be conscious of it wherever you go and whatever you may be doing. Know assuredly the Almighty God is with you. Whether in the open or in the secret; when the going is good and when it is rough: He is there. The thought of this will keep you holy. You do not want to sin right in His presence because you love, honour and fear Him. It will also produce strong faith and great boldness in you. There is nothing impossible to God, and since He is with you nothing is impossible to you. It should also give you the assurance of victory in all your encounters with the enemy. The One who is with and in you is greater than he who is in the world. Count on it: God is with you. The thought of it should make you strong.

Secondly, you should see to it that you do not break the hedge and grieve God, who is always there. The presence of God with you creates a hedge around you, protecting you from all evil and satanic attacks. As long as the hedge remains intact there is nothing the devil can do. But when the hedge is broken, the enemy can then creep in to attack. *'Whoso breaketh an hedge, a serpent shall bite him'* (Ecclesiastes 10:8b). The hedge is broken by sin, disobedience or rebellion. Sin, no matter how small, leaves enough opening for that old serpent unless the blood of Jesus is quickly applied to your life again. Beware of the danger of sin. Keep the enemy out. Enjoy the divine presence.

The battle may be fierce, but our victory is certain. The adversaries may be many but *'fear not: for they that be with us are more than they that be with them'* (II Kings 6:16).

Our Lord is with us to fight for us, to save us, to deliver us. Have faith. Be strong. Be true, and faithful unto death. One day we shall wear the Overcomers' crown and rejoice for ever and ever.

Be strong and courageous, be not afraid nor dismayed . . . for all the multitude that is with him: for there be more with us than with him: with him is an arm of flesh; but with us is the LORD our God to help us, and to fight our battles.

(II Chronicles 32:7–8)

Have not I commanded thee? Be strong and of a good courage; be not afraid, neither be thou dismayed: for the LORD thy God is with thee whithersoever thou goest.

(Joshua 1:9)

JESUS IS LORD!

Notes

Chapter 1

1. E. W. Kenyon, *The Wonderful Name of Jesus* p. 19.

Chapter 6

1. This is implied from the Scriptures. Historically, before the heathen Philistines went to battle, they worshipped and sacrificed in the house of their gods, inviting the assistance of evil spirits.

Chapter 8

1. W. E. Vine, Challenge, 1977. An *Expository Dictionary of New Testament Words* p 97.
2. E. W. Kenyon, *Two Kinds of Faith.*

Chapter 11

1. Luis Palau, *Moment to Shout.*

Teaching Tapes (Audio)
By
Francis Wale Oke

Arise And Shine
Absolute Victory
A Change Of Identity
Bringing Down The Glory
The Snare Is Broken
Turn To The Rock And Drink
Let Us Pass Over Unto The Other Side
Is Your Name Written In The Book Of Life?
The Danger Of Compromise
Let The Fire Fall
Walking In God's Covenant
From Curses To Blessing
The Pursuit Of Holiness
Anointing For Wealth
Christian Dressing
Divine Intervention
3-Dimension Of Warfare
Family Life I, II, III.
Overwelming Anointing.

Teaching Tapes (Video)
By
Francis Wale Oke

Bringing Down the Glory
New Wine For Your Life
Victory By Your Right Hand
The Pursuit Of Holiness
Anointed With Fresh Oil
Overwhelming Anointing
From Curses To Blessings
A New Anointing
The Power To Get Wealth
Walking In God's Covenant
From Glory To Glory
The Glory Of The Latter House
The Blessings Of Abraham
Moving With The Cloud Of Glory
The Foundation For An Effective Ministry
Power In The Word
Let The Fire Fall

Order All Materials From:

Nigeria:
The Sword of the Spirit Ministries
P.O. Box 6308 Agodi P.O.,
Ibadan.
Tel. 034 22 710830.
Telex: 31503 SOTSM NG.

United Kingdom:
The Sword of the Spirit Ministries
P.O. Box 2559,
London NW11 0QQ
or
25 Belmont Avenue,
London N17 6AX.
Tel. 081 881 7027.

United States & Canada:
Christ Life Church
2653 Seagird B/vd
Appt #6c far Rockaway
New York 11691.
Tel: 718 327 0627